Xinghui Huang
Roberto Horowitz

Robust Control of Dual-Stage Servo Systems in Hard Disk
Drives

Xinghui Huang
Roberto Horowitz

Robust Control of Dual-Stage Servo Systems in Hard Disk Drives

Methodology Development, Comparative Study, and Experimental Verification

VDM Verlag Dr. Müller

Imprint

Bibliographic information by the German National Library: The German National Library lists this publication at the German National Bibliography; detailed bibliographic information is available on the Internet at http://dnb.d-nb.de.

Cover image: www.purestockx.com

Publisher:
VDM Verlag Dr. Müller Aktiengesellschaft & Co. KG , Dudweiler Landstr. 125 a, 66123 Saarbrücken, Germany,
Phone +49 681 9100-698, Fax +49 681 9100-988,
Email: info@vdm-verlag.de

Zugl.: Berkeley, University of California at Berkeley, Diss., 2006

Produced in USA and UK by:
Lightning Source Inc., La Vergne, Tennessee, USA
Lightning Source UK Ltd., Milton Keynes, UK
BookSurge LLC, 5341 Dorchester Road, Suite 16, North Charleston, SC 29418, USA

ISBN: 978-3-639-01507-2

Preface

In order to sustain the continuing increase in data storage density in magnetic hard disk drives (HDDs), high-bandwidth dual-stage actuator servo systems have been developed to improve the accuracy of read/write head positioning. In this work, robust track-following control design methodologies and algorithms are developed for dual-stage servo systems with a MEMS microactuator (MA) and an instrumented suspension equipped with a vibration sensor. After a detailed overview of advanced servo systems used in current hard disk drives, modeling and robust control designs based on single-input single-output (SISO) and multi-input multi-output (MIMO) configurations are presented. Detailed analysis and comparisons are made between various designs. Experimental control results are presented for a prototype microactuator fabricated using MEMS techniques. This book is intended to serve as a reference to robust servo design techniques for graduate students in Controls, servo engineers in the hard disk drive industry, and anyone else who may be considering designing robust, multi-objective, and multirate controllers in various applications.

The book is organized as follows. Chapter 1 gives a detailed overview of advanced servo systems used in recent hard disk drives. In Chapter 2, a complete numerical model is constructed for the dual-stage system. This model includes the following features: the coupling dynamics of the MA, airflow excited MA vibration and suspension vibration, and quantitative parametric and dynamic uncertainties. These features make the model more realistic for controller design and performance evaluation through simulation. Chapters 3 and 4 present robust track-following controllers designs based on both sequential SISO design techniques and robust MIMO design techniques, respectively. Multirate sensing is incorporated in both SISO and MIMO designs. Simulations are conducted to verify the effectiveness of these designs. The differences between rotational and translational MAs are investigated in Chapter 5, especially in suspension vibration attenuation. Detailed comparisons between these methodologies are made in terms of nominal performance, robust stability, robust performance, and implementation costs. Guidelines to practical implementation of these designs are also summarized. In Chapter 6, A prototype dual-stage system is tested and identified. The MA coupling dynamics are experimentally checked, and the level of airflow excited MA vibration is estimated, validating the MA model and the disturbance model used in the simulation study. A preliminary controller is designed to show the functionality of the dual-stage system with only one output. This work lays the basis for future design for a fully functional dual-stage system when the suspension vibration information and the MA relative motion are also measurable.

We wish to express our appreciation to Professors Masayoshi Tomizuka and Laurent El Ghaoui for their valuable suggestions for the book. Our special thanks go to Professor Ryozo Nagamune, University of British Columbia, for his valuable contributions and collaborative research on multirate control; Professor Kenn Oldham, Michigan University, for his supply of prototype MEMS microactuators; Dr. Yunfeng Li, Samsung Information Storage of America, for his great help on disk drive control design and implementation. We would also like to thank the following people: Stanley Kon; Jongeun Choi, Michigan State University; and Xiaotian Sun, Hitachi Global Storage Technology, for their valuable support and advice.

Seagate Technology, Pittsburgh, PA   Xinghui Huang
University of California at Berkeley, Berkeley, CA   Roberto Horowitz
April 2008

Contents

Chapter 1

Introduction

Magnetic hard disk drives (HDDs) have been widely used in commercial computer systems like PCs and high-end servers for many years. From the recent years, they have also been applied in many consumer electronics like digital music players, digital cameras, cell phones, and video-cameras. They are continuously evolving to achieve higher storage capacity and miniaturized sizes. Fig. 1.1 shows the schematic of a typical hard disk drive system. It mainly consists of a spindle motor, one or more disks with data written on their surfaces, heads/sliders, suspensions, arms (E-blocks), and a voice-coil motor (VCM). During operation, the spindle motor spins the disk as fast as 10,000 RPM and generates high speed airflow between the slider and the disk surface. This high speed airflow has the effect of air bearing to balance the pre-load force from the suspension. The dynamic balance can keep the slider at a constant flying height of several nanometers over the contours of the disk surface regardless of its undulation and roughness. The VCM moves its arm by rotating the E-block around its pivot and positions the head at the right radial location for data reading from or writing to disk data tracks.

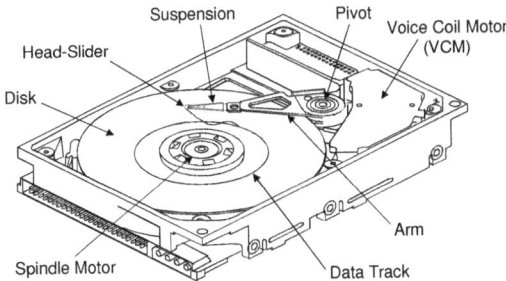

Figure 1.1: Schematic of a hard disk drive

1.1   Track Mis-Registration and Position Error Signal

In modern disk drives, each disk has concentric tracks on its surface. For proper functioning of a disk drive system, it should be able to precisely position the read/write head on the desired track. Some terminologies are needed to characterize the tracking performance, one of which is write-to-read track mis-registration (TMR). Write-to-read TMR is defined as the offset between the pass of the read head (read track) and the pass of a written track [63]. Small TMR is desirable since large TMR can cause reading of erroneous information.

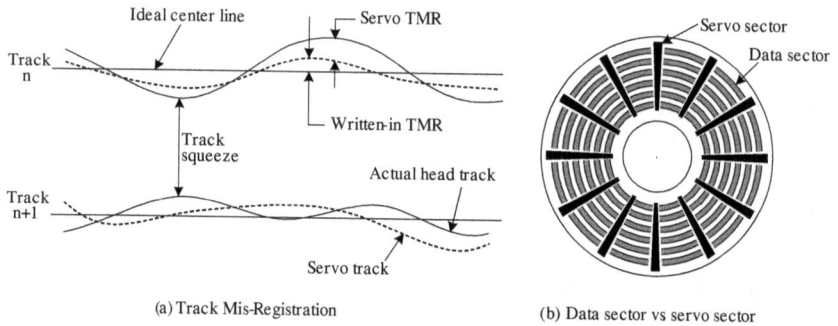

(a) Track Mis-Registration

(b) Data sector vs servo sector

Figure 1.2: Track mis-registration and servo sector

However, write-to-read TMR cannot be measured directly in modern disk drives. Instead, it is quantified by servo TMR, which is often simply called TMR and is defined by the statistical distribution of the deviation of the head position from the position of the desired servo track. This deviation is also called the position error signal (PES) and is obtained by reading out the encoded position information on servo sectors. If the PES is assumed to have a Gaussian distribution, then TMR can be represented by three times the standard deviation of the PES, i.e., 3σ PES. Since servo sectors are evenly embedded in data tracks at discrete locations, the PES is sampled at a fixed frequency that is determined by the disk rotation speed and the number of servo sectors per revolution. Given the disk rotation speed, a higher PES sampling frequency requires more servo sectors per revolution and reduces data storage efficiency.

There are many sources contributing to TMR. A thorough understanding of these sources is critical to come up with solutions to reducing these contributions. Typically, TMR can be classified as two main categories: repeatable runout (RRO) and non-repeatable runout (NRRO). RRO is related to spindle and disk rotation, and is hence synchronous with the disk rotation speed. The main cause of RRO is disk slippage which results in track circle eccentricity during disk rotation. Another important source of RRO is written-in TMR which results in track circle imperfection. Among TMR, all other contributions except RRO are classified as NRRO. Primary NRRO contributors include the following [9][15][55][14]: spindle runout, disk flutter, seek settling runout, flex cable bias force, external shock and vibrations, PES demodulation and quantization noise, DAC quantization noise, etc.

1.2 Basic Servo Architecture

Since the first HDD was invented in the 1950s by IBM, disk drives' data storage areal density has been following Moore's law, doubling roughly every 18 months [1] [63]. The current storage density is about 230 giga-bit per square inch, as reported by Hitachi GST [18]. A goal of the magnetic disk drive industry is to break the storage density barrier of 1 terabit per square inch. It is widely accepted that the necessary track density for achieving this target will be about 500,000 tracks per inch (TPI). Assuming TMR (3σ PES) is required to be less than 10% of the track pitch width, we conclude that a TMR budget of less than 5 nm is necessary to achieve this track density. This TMR budget poses a stringent requirement on the performance of disk drive servo systems under various disturbances, such as track runout, windage, bias force, and external shock and vibration.

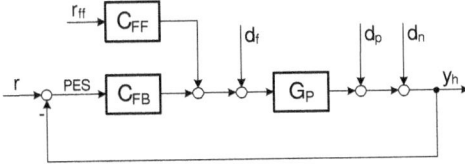

Figure 1.3: Disk drive servo architecture

A disk drive servo system has two major tasks: track seeking and track following. In track seeking, the read/write head is moved from the current track to a desired track as quickly as possible. Any shock or overshoot resulting from the seeking process should decay quickly so that data writing or reading can start early. In track following, the head is kept as close as possible to the track center so that data writing or reading can proceed with an acceptable error rate. On the other hand, smaller tracking error allows more data tracks to be put within a given radial width, thus achieving higher track density.

Fig. 1.3 shows the block diagram of a disk drive servo system. In the figure, G_P represents the actuator plant, C_{FB} is the feedback controller. d_n, d_f, and d_p denote measurement noise, force/torque disturbance, and track position disturbance, respectively. r denotes the reference input, which is a designed position trajectory in the track-seeking mode, and zero in the track-following mode. r_{ff} is a reference input to the feedforward controller C_{FF}. r_{ff} can be the desired trajectory r in the track-seeking mode, and/or some auxiliary information such as acceleration resulting from external shock or vibrations.

The performance and specifications of a disk drive servo system can be most effectively embodied by the sensitivity function, also called the error rejection function, of the

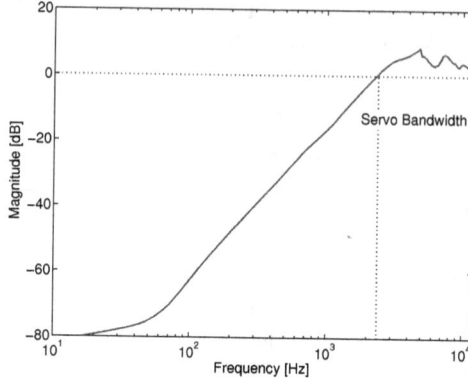

Figure 1.4: Sensitivity function frequency response

closed-loop system, which is defined by

$$S(z) = \frac{1}{1 + C_{FB}(z)G_P(z)}. \tag{1.1}$$

Note that the system has been treated as a discrete-time system to account for its digital control property. The typical frequency response of a sensitivity function is shown in Fig. 1.4. Some features are common for sensitivity functions. It has low gain below zero dB in the low frequency range, and has gain above zero dB in the high frequency range. Ideally, we want to have more attenuation in the low frequency range since the major TMR sources are located in that range, and to suppress amplification in the high frequency range since measurement noises and uncertain dynamics of the plant are mostly located in the high frequency range. The frequency point with zero dB is related to the servo bandwidth of the control system. However, according to Bode's sensitivity integral theorem [5][39], the sensitivity response curve cannot be suppressed over the whole frequency range and has to satisfy the following constraint

$$\int_0^\infty \log |S(j\omega)| \mathrm{d}\omega = 0, \quad \text{(continuous-time)},$$

$$\int_0^\pi \log \left| S(e^{j\theta}) \right| \mathrm{d}\theta = 0, \quad \text{(discrete-time)}. \tag{1.2}$$

This relation implies that pushing down the curve at some frequency range is achieved at the cost of bouncing up the curve at some other frequency range. This effect is also called the water-bed effect. For a disk drive servo system, the whole frequency range is bounded by the Nyquist frequency which is half of the PES sampling frequency. A higher PES sampling frequency allows for a higher Nyquist frequency, therefore more error rejection can be achieved without too much amplification in the high frequency region. However, as mentioned before, the PES sampling frequency is fixed for given disk drive specifications, since a higher sampling frequency reduces data storage efficiency.

With a fixed PES sampling frequency, a careful tradeoff has to be made between low frequency error rejection and high frequency noise/uncertainty amplification. If the closed-loop bandwidth is pushed too high, then the frequencies for gain margin and/or phase margin will be placed close to the suspension's first major resonance mode at about 4~5 kHz. This is undesirable since the system's stability will be greatly affected by the variation of that suspension resonance mode. Ideally the sensitivity response should be optimally shaped such that the overall tracking error can be minimized while still retaining sufficient stability margin with respect to the plant uncertainty range that is known or estimated *a priori*.

1.3 Advanced Servo Systems

1.3.1 Dual-Stage Actuation

Actuated Suspension [30][11][6][2]

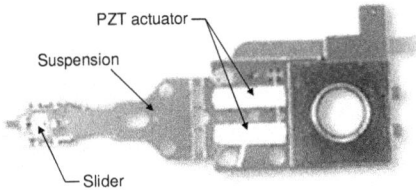

Figure 1.5: PZT-actuated suspension

Fig. 1.5 shows an example of actuated suspensions. In this structure, two piezoelectric elements are attached to each carriage arm. The two PZT elements, polarized in opposite directions, are mounted in parallel around a baseplate hinge. The top surfaces of the two PZT elements are electrically connected by a wire and the bottom surface of each PZT element is adhesively bonded to the baseplate hinge. When a voltage is applied to both single-ended PZT elements, one PZT element extends, and the other one contracts. The push-pull actuation of the two PZT elements displaces the head in the off-track direction.

Since active off-track motion is generated by the PZT actuators through the suspension, those suspension modes can still be excited during actuation. The phase delay of the PZT actuator dynamics prevents the dual-stage system from achieving much wider servo bandwidth. PZT-actuated suspensions are usually designed to have a relatively low frequency sway mode in order to increase the actuation gain and to reduce the driving voltage. This makes the suspensions more susceptible to airflow turbulence excitation than their conventional counterparts.

Actuated Slider/Head-Gimbal Assembly [19][46]

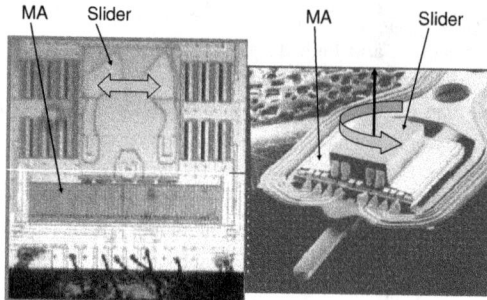

Figure 1.6: MEMS microactuators, translational vs. rotational

To reduce the excitation of suspension modes by a PZT actuator, the PZT elements can be moved closer to the head-gimbal assembly (HGA) and only the HGA is moved during actuation. This makes the PZT elements smaller and the head off-track motion can be generated by the PZT actuator more directly. However, some suspension modes may still be excited by the PZT elements due to the not-so-small moving inertia of the HGA.

An improved approach to solving the above problem is to place a microactuator (MA) between the gimbal and slider, then the moving mass of the MA can be reduced to the slider mass only. This MA is usually of electrostatic type fabricated using MEMS techniques. Two MEMS MA examples are shown in Fig. 1.6.

This kind of MAs can be either rotational or translational, and they usually have a single mode of 1~3 kHz and have a clean dynamic response up to 20 kHz. Due to its small moving inertia, a rotational MA can be viewed as decoupled with the VCM since the slider is mounted on the MA in such a way that its center of mass coincides with the MA's axis of in-plane rotation. Then the slider's rotation momentum resulting by MA actuation can be neglected compared to the VCM's swinging motion with much larger rotation momentum. Due to this decoupling property, rotational MAs are suitable for track seeking since independent motion can be generated by both the VCM and MA and contributes to the desired track trajectory effectively. However, in a track-following process, the rotational MA has to compensate for the head's position error induced by suspension vibrations without any passive attenuation.

On the other hand, a translational MA has inherent coupling dynamics with the VCM, since translational motion at the suspension tip can excite the MA dynamics through its mass-spring-damper structure. Mechanical, or passive, attenuation of suspension vibrations is therefore possible if the MA has a lower resonance frequency than those suspension modes, which is usually the case. Due to the coupling property, a translational MA should be carefully protected in a track-seeking process, since significant acceleration and hence inertial force generated by the VCM may push/pull the MA's moving part to its critical region, where an undesirable phenomenon called pull-in may result.

Actuated Head [57][38]

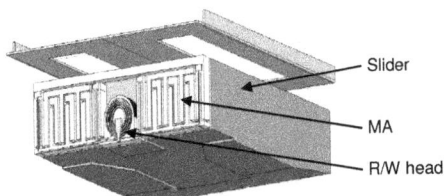

Figure 1.7: Actuated read/write head, by H. Toshiyoshi

In the actuated head approach, an MA is integrated into the slider structure and moves only the read/write head. With much smaller moving inertia compared to both an actuated suspension and an actuated slider, the actuated head type MA has a much higher bandwidth of up to 30 kHz and a working stroke of 0.5 μm . This implies little coupling between the VCM and MA, since the VCM dynamics are usually in a frequency range below 15 kHz. However, the integration of the slider, the MA, and the read/write head remains a challenge.

1.3.2 Multi-Sensing and Multirate Control

As mentioned before, the PES has a limited sampling frequency which is determined by the disk rotation speed and the number of servo sectors per revolution. Since the PES contains error resulting from various kinds of disturbance sources, attenuation of a specific disturbance source, e.g., airflow excited suspension vibration, is not possible with this information only. Low frequency error compensation and high frequency noise rejection cannot be achieved simultaneously according to Bode's integral theorem, and a tradeoff has to be made between them. A solution to this problem is to implement multi-sensing by adding auxiliary sensors to the servo system. Two main proposals have been explored: external disturbance rejection by acceleration feedforward compensation and suspension vibration attenuation by active damping.

In the first approach, accelerometers are placed on the base plate of the disk drive to detect external shock or vibration [3][23][43][49][59]. The detected information is then fed to a compensator which moves the actuator to cancel the effect of external disturbances before they affect the head off-track position. Due to the phase-lead property of acceleration compared to both velocity and position, this control mechanism is feedforward control and has very good effect.

The second approach utilizes the information from the strain sensors fabricated on the suspension surface to actively damp some major suspension modes [28][35]. As mentioned before, servo bandwidth cannot be further increased due to the presence of suspension resonance modes, especially the butterfly mode which usually has a high peak and a relatively low resonance frequency. By damping one or more major suspension modes, the servo system is made more robust to mode variation, and therefore it is possible to further expand the servo bandwidth.

With more signals available by multi-sensing, it is desirable to utilize them in a proper way such that the contained information can be fully exploited. Unlike the PES, which has a fixed sampling frequency, these auxiliary signals can be sampled at a higher rate than that of the PES. High rate sampling is desirable for handling high frequency disturbances such as airflow excited suspension vibrations. This leads to a scheme called multirate control, in which two or more different rates are applied in either control updating or sensor signal sampling, depending on the system configuration. Computation saving may also be achieved, since a low rate can be applied to update the slow components of a compound signal [62].

1.4   Overview of Dual-Stage Control Design Methodologies

Various control design architectures and methodologies have been developed for the control design of dual-stage servo systems. They can be largely classified into two categories: those based on decoupled or sequential single-input single-output (SISO) designs, and those based on modern optimal design methodologies, such as LQG/LTR [22], μ-synthesis [17][32], and mixed H_2/H_∞. Two constraints must be considered in the dual-stage servo control design. First, the motion contribution from each actuator must be properly allocated. Usually, the first-stage actuator, or the coarse actuator, has a large moving range with low bandwidth, while the second-stage actuator, or the fine actuator, has high bandwidth with a small moving range. So the fine actuator tries its best to work in a high frequency range without saturation, while the coarse actuator works in the remaining low frequency range with a much larger stroke. Second, the destructive effect, in which the two actuators fight each other by moving in opposite directions, must be avoided. This is especially an issue for SISO design methodologies, since each control loop is designed sequentially without systematic optimization between them. However, most MIMO design methodologies can take this problem into account naturally by taking control effort as an objective during minimization.

1.4.1   Classical SISO Design Methodologies

Several architectures and design methodologies have been proposed to transform the dual-stage control design problem into a decoupled or sequential SISO compensators design problem, for example, master-slave design, decoupling design, parallel design and PQ method. Fig. 1.8 shows the block diagrams for various dual-stage control design methods.

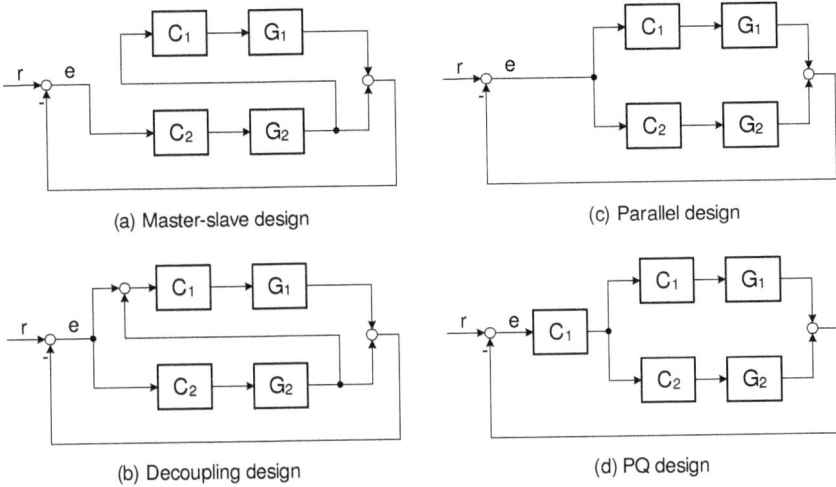

(a) Master-slave design   (c) Parallel design

(b) Decoupling design   (d) PQ design

Figure 1.8: Various SISO design structures

In these subfigures, G_1 and G_2 represent the coarse actuator (VCM) and fine actuator (mini- or microactuator) respectively. r is the reference input and e denotes the position error.

In a traditional master-slave structure, the position error is first compensated for by the high-bandwidth fine actuator, and the coarse actuator follows the fine actuator to avoid its saturation. The decoupling design method achieves sensitivity decoupling by adding the relative motion output from the fine actuator to the position error, to generate the position error of the coarse actuator relative to the track. Details of the track-following control design using this method will be discussed in section 3.2. It is also possible to design a dual-stage controller directly by using a parallel structure. Some design constraints are first imposed, then sequential loop closing can be conducted [53]. However, a more straightforward way for such a design idea is the PQ method [51], in which the virtual plant G_1/G_2 is first stabilized by a compensator C_1/C_2 in order to optimize controller interference. Then C_0 is designed to close the partially designed plant $C_1G_1 + C_2G_2$. Details about this design method will be presented in section 3.3.

1.4.2   Modern MIMO Design Methodologies

A common feature of SISO design methodologies is that the originally MIMO dual-stage plant should first be artificially decoupled into two subsystems, G_1 and G_2. Inherent coupling in the system is therefore lost after this manipulation. In this aspect, MIMO design methodologies perform better than SISO counterparts. Quite a few modern MIMO optimal design methodologies have been applied in the design of dual-stage controllers.

Based on conventional LQG control, the method of linear quadratic Gaussian / loop-transfer recovery (LQG/LTR) tries to recover robustness from pure LQG by a Kalman filter redesign process [22]. μ-synthesis explicitly considers robust stability using μ with the condition that system performance should also be expressed by H_∞ norms which is somewhat unnatural [36]. Mixed H_2/H_∞ performs H_2 norm optimization with some H_∞ bounds to guarantee robust stability [54][25]. An improved version of mixed H_2/H_∞ is mixed H_2/μ [27], which characterizes robust stability more precisely at the cost of an increased controller order. Structured uncertainty can therefore be considered in mixed H_2/μ rather than in mixed H_2/H_∞. Both of the two design methods only optimize the nominal performance. In robust H_2 [42], the worst-case performance is directly optimized with respect to parametric uncertainties. These three multi-objective design methods will be discussed in detail in chapter 4.

1.5 Research Objectives

To further increase the information storage density in HDDs, dual-stage actuators have been proposed as a viable solution to improving the performance of disk drive servos. Auxiliary vibration sensors have also been proposed for airflow excited suspension vibration detection and compensation. The dual-stage system with an instrumented suspension is a typical MIMO system: it has two control inputs to the VCM and MA respectively, the PES as the main measurement, and two auxiliary signals: the strain sensor signal and the relative motion of the MA. Multivariable design approaches with multirate sensing and control incorporated are therefore necessary to exploit the system capability as much as possible. On the other hand, plant uncertainty and variation impose new challenges to the design of robust HDD servo systems. Robust stability and robust performance should be explicitly considered in the design process, so that the final servo system performs well on a huge batch of disk drives with slightly different dynamics. Not much attention has been paid to the two issues in previous work. The first objective of this dissertation is therefore to develop robust, multirate, and adaptive controller design methodologies for dual-stage servo systems, and to investigate the advantages and disadvantages of these methodologies with guidelines for practical implementation.

A general dual-stage plant model is constructed, which consists of a multi-mode instrumented suspension and a rotational/translational MEMS MA. Various disturbance sources are modelled, including airflow disturbance sources acting on the suspension. Quantitative dynamic and parametric uncertainties are modeled, which will be explicitly considered in design processes, and also will be used to check the performance and robustness of closed-loop systems.

Two sequential SISO design methodologies, the sensitivity decoupling (SD) method and the PQ method, and three MIMO design ones: mixed H_2/H_∞, mixed H_2/μ and robust H_2, will be investigated. Detailed comparisons are made between the rotational and translational MAs, between all of these robust multirate designs with respect to performance, robust stability, and robust performance, and also between various sensing schemes of the plant.

The second objective of this book is to experimentally test the behavior, dynamics, and to demonstrate the performance of a recently built dual-stage actuator with a translational MEMS MA. System identification is performed. Airflow excited MA vibration and suspension vibration are observed and estimated. Without suspension vibration sensors and an MA capacitive sensor, preliminary control design is conducted using the PQ method, and the resulting closed-loop system is tested.

1.6   Outline of this Book

This book is organized as follows. Chapter 2 presents the modeling of a generalized dual-stage actuator with a MEMS microactuator and instrumented suspension. Plant uncertainty is also modeled for the design that follows. Chapters 3 and 4 discuss the controller design for the modeled dual-stage system. In Chapter 3, two SISO design methods, the SD method and the PQ method, are discussed. Chapter 4 presents three multi-objective optimization methods: mixed H_2/H_∞, mixed H_2/μ, and robust H_2. Multirate sensing and multirate control are incorporated in the design in a systematic way. Their advantages and disadvantages are also discussed. Chapter 5 presents detailed comparisons between different plant configurations, between SISO and MIMO design results, and between different sensing schemes. The feasibility of performance projection to 500k TPI with various technical improvements is also explored in that chapter.

Chapter 6 presents the testing, modeling of a prototype dual-stage actuator with a MEMS microactuator. Controller design by the PQ method and testing results are then presented.

Chapter 7 concludes this book by summarizing the results and major achievements. Recommendations of future work are also discussed.

Chapter 2

Modeling of a Generalized Dual-Stage Servo System with a MEMS Microactuator and an Instrumented Suspension

2.1 The Nominal Plant

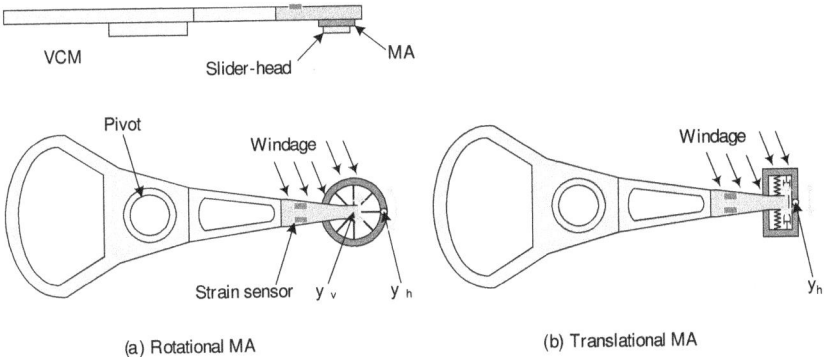

(a) Rotational MA

(b) Translational MA

Figure 2.1: Schematic of rotational and translational MAs

Fig. 2.1 shows the schematic of dual-stage systems with a MEMS MA and an instrumented suspension. As illustrated in the figure, the MA motion type, either rotational or translational, is defined for the head motion with respect to its center of mass, which coincides with the suspension tip. Strain sensors are fabricated on the suspension surface for the detection of suspension vibration. In the track-following mode, the suspension tip motion, which is also rotational with respect to the pivot center, is much larger than the MA motion, and hence can be viewed as translational in both cases. Airflow turbulence, also called windage, acts on the suspension and the MA when the slider-head assembly is flying over the rotating disk. Suspension vibration modes can be excited by airflow turbulence, and this is a main contributor to suspension vibration and hence head vibration.

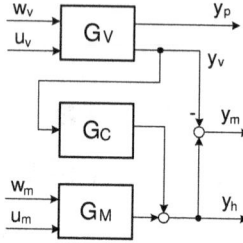

Figure 2.2: Block diagram of the dual-stage actuator with a rotational/translational MA

A block diagram for the dual-stage system is shown in Fig. 2.2. In that figure, G_V and G_M represent the dynamics of the VCM and MA respectively. u_v and u_m are the control inputs, and w_v and w_m are the airflow disturbances to the VCM and MA, respectively. y_h, y_p, y_m, and y_v are the read/write head position, the strain sensor output, the relative motion output of the MA, and the suspension tip displacement, respectively. y_m is also called the relative position error signal (RPES). In conventional single-stage disk drive systems, only y_h is available in the form of the PES by retrieving position information from servo sectors on the disk and comparing it with the desired head position. In dual-stage systems with a MEMS MA and an instrumented suspension, y_p and y_m are also measurable from the strain sensor on the suspension and the capacitive sensor embedded in the MA structure, respectively. In single-stage systems, y_v is equivalent to y_h, since y_m is always zero; while in dual-stage systems, y_v is not measurable.

Typically, the VCM-suspension assembly consists of a major flex cable mode, several arm modes, and a number of suspension resonance modes. The transfer function from u_v to y_v can be expressed as

$$G_V(s) = \sum_{i=0}^{N} \frac{A_i}{s^2 + 2\zeta_i \omega_i s + \omega_i^2}, \tag{2.1}$$

where for each mode i, A_i is the modal constant, ζ_i is the damping ratio, and ω_i is the resonance frequency. In this parametric model, mode 0 denotes the flex cable mode around 100 Hz. There is a major arm sway mode at 7.4 kHz, which is also called the butterfly mode, and five suspension resonance modes at 5.1 kHz, 9.1 kHz, 10.7 kHz, 13 kHz, and 15 kHz, respectively. All these resonance modes have a light damping coefficient of about 0.015 N·s/m. During disk rotation, high-speed airflow turbulence in the disk drive enclosure impinges on the suspension and excites suspension vibrations. Each suspension mode is excited by an independent windage source, and the strain sensor picks up vibration information from each mode with another set of values for A_i as those in (2.1).

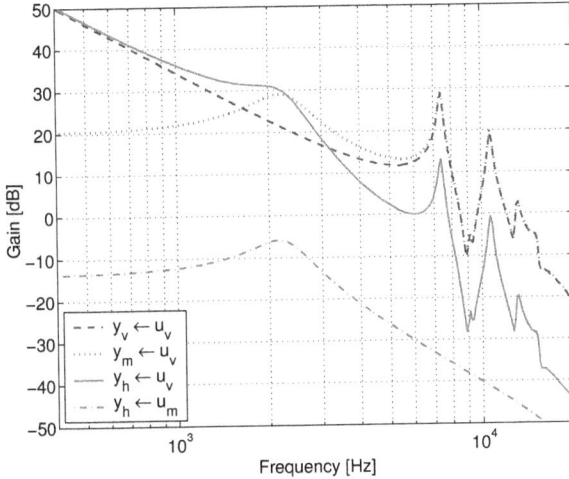

Figure 2.3: Frequency responses of the dual-stage actuator with a rotational/translational MA

The MA dynamics can be modeled as a single spring-mass-damper system with the following transfer function from either u_m or w_m to y_h

$$G_M(s) = \frac{A_m}{s^2 + 2\zeta_m \omega_m s + \omega_m^2}. \qquad (2.2)$$

Usually ω_m is designed to be about 1~2 kHz, and ζ_m is about 0.1 N·s/m. u_m and w_m are both force inputs but with different values for A_m.

G_C is the coupling dynamics from y_v to y_h. When the MA is rotational, the slider is usually mounted on the MA in such a way that its center of mass coincides with the actuator's axis of in-plane rotation. Then any translational motion of the suspension tip generated by the VCM cannot excite any rotational motion of the MA. In this case, G_C is constantly one, and y_m is solely the output of the MA driven by u_m, implying virtually no coupling between the VCM and MA [34]. In the translational MA case, we have a coupled dual-stage system. G_C is then derived from the MA dynamics and can be expressed as

$$G_C(s) = \frac{2\zeta_m \omega_m s + \omega_m^2}{s^2 + 2\zeta_m \omega_m s + \omega_m^2}. \qquad (2.3)$$

This coupling effect implies that the VCM actuation will excite the dynamics of the MA, and y_m becomes the combined output of all inputs including u_v, u_m, and windage w_v and w_m. In both cases, rotational and translational, actuation of the MA can be assumed to have little effect on the VCM dynamics due to the very small inertia of the MA compared to that of the VCM. This assumption implies that the transfer function from u_m to y_p is constantly zero.

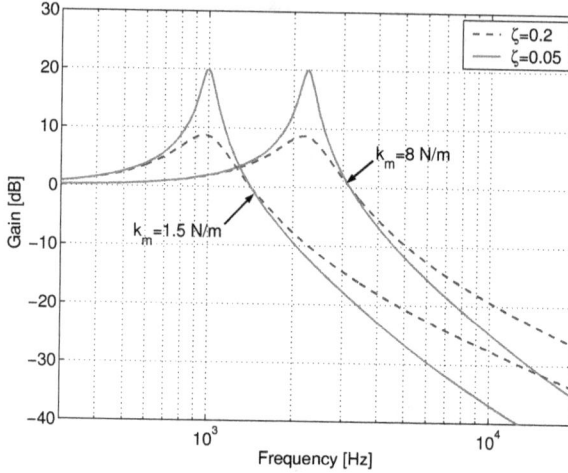

Figure 2.4: Frequency responses of the coupling dynamics G_C

In the translational MA case, the coupling dynamics exhibit a low-pass filtering effect, as shown in Fig. 2.4. It can be seen that both the spring stiffness k_m and the damping coefficient c_m can influence the filtering effect. This effect makes a difference between the rotational and translational MAs. From the viewpoint of suspension vibration attenuation, a soft spring and a light damping effect are desired, since most high frequency suspension vibrations can be attenuated when passing through the MA. On the other hand, we want large values for k_m and c_m, so that the transfer function from u_v to y_h has high gain in a wide frequency range for effective track-following control. Therefore a trade-off is necessary between suspension vibration attenuation and track following. From Fig. 2.4 we can see that, when ω_m=2.2 kHz and $\zeta_m = 0.2$, the gain of G_C is above zero dB up to 3 kHz, implying little degradation of the actuation gain of the VCM-suspension assembly in the low frequency range for track following, and adequate filtering in the high frequency range for suspension vibration attenuation.

For clarity, we define G_H to be the transfer function from u_v to y_h, then from Fig. 2.2 we have

$$G_H = G_C G_V. \tag{2.4}$$

2.2   Disturbance Characterization

There are various types of disturbances entering the servo system of a disk drive. Many research results on disturbances characterization and suppression have been reported in the literature [64][9][15][14][12]. The disturbances entering the servo system can be roughly categorized into three types:

Torque disturbances, which include D/A quantization noise, power-amp noise, bearing imperfection and nonlinearity, flex cable bias, and especially high frequency airflow turbulence impinging on the suspension-slider assembly;

Track runout, which includes nonrepeatable motion of the disk such as spindle bearing imperfection and disk flutter, and repeatable track motion such as eccentricity due to disk slippage and imperfection of track circles due to written-in TMR;

Noises, which include PES demodulation noise, sensor noises, electrical noise, and A/D quantization noise.

For the purpose of servo control design, the disturbances are modeled as follows. The reference signal, r, includes track runout and the head motion resulting from all torque disturbances, except the airflow turbulence acting on the two actuators. A third order model is used to characterize its low frequency feature

$$
\begin{aligned}
r(s) &= W_r(s)w_r(s) \\
&= \left(\frac{7.8 \times 10^9}{s^2 + 800s + 2.5 \times 10^5} + \frac{1.2 \times 10^5}{s + 1.9 \times 10^3} \right) w_r(s) \,,
\end{aligned}
\tag{2.5}
$$

where $W_r(s)$ is the weighting function for track runout, and w_r is a normalized white noise with a Gaussian distribution and zero mean. The RMS value of this runout is about 450 nm in the range of 5 Hz~25 kHz.

The airflow turbulence impinging on the two actuators is respectively denoted as w_v and w_m. Each suspension mode has an independent disturbance source which is assumed to be white. Therefore, w_v is a vector containing all of these mode disturbances and w_m is a scalar. In this model, the airflow excited suspension vibration has an RMS value of about 5 nm, and of about 4 nm for w_m excited MA vibration. The three signals, PES, y_p and y_m, have their corresponding measurement noises with the RMS values of 1 nm, 0.1 nm and 1 nm, respectively. In practice, they should be properly estimated and modeled, so that the servo designed based on the modeled system can achieve the optimal performance during practical implementation.

2.3   Plant Uncertainty

Plant uncertainty is inherent in all dynamic systems. Hard disk drives are typically fabricated in a huge batch, and each drive has slightly different dynamic properties with the same nominal properties. When servo control is embedded in disk drive systems, it is infeasible to fine tune controller parameters for each individual disk drive. Therefore the same controller should stabilize and perform well on all these disk drives. This raises the issue of stability robustness and performance robustness of disk drive servo systems. In this section, various types of plant uncertainties are modeled for the dual-stage system, so that stability robustness and/or performance robustness can later on be implicitly or explicitly considered in controller design and closed-loop system analysis.

Table 2.1: Parameter Variation Ranges

	A	ζ	ω
G_V	±5%	±20%	± 8%
G_M	±5%	±20%	±12%

2.3.1 Parametric Uncertainty

Since the dual-stage model is expressed as a combination of both suspension and MA modes, and each mode is characterized by three parameters (i.e., A, ζ, ω), it is natural to consider parametric uncertainty for both control design and performance evaluation. We assume that the variation range of each parameter with respect to its nominal value is as specified in Table 2.1. As well known, parametric uncertainty can be represented using linear fractional transformation (LFT) [4]. For example, suppose there is a ±10% variation in parameter a, then the actual value a_a can be represented in terms of its nominal value a_n and that variation range using the following LFT

$$a_a = F_L(A_a, \delta_a) = F_L\left(\begin{bmatrix} a_n & 0.1a_n \\ 1 & 0 \end{bmatrix}, \delta_a\right), \tag{2.6}$$

where F_L indicates that the lower loop of the matrix is closed with δ_a, and δ_a is a real-valued perturbation with $|\delta_a| \leq 1$.

Repeatedness of MA Parametric Uncertainties

It is noted that, for a translational MA, the coupling part, G_C, shares the same resonance mode with G_M. Furthermore, the numerator of G_C is derived from its denominator, or its characteristic polynomial. So, when varying ω_m and ζ_m of the MA mode, both the numerator and denominator of G_C will be varied, resulting in repeated (twice) uncertainties for the MA's parameters. This phenomenon is illustrated in Fig. 2.5 for a standard mode representation

$$G(s) = \frac{b_0}{s^2 + a_1 s + a_0}. \tag{2.7}$$

In that figure, each parameter has been represented using LFT as defined in (2.6). The information of repeatedness of uncertainties will be utilized in μ analysis later on.

2.3.2 Multiplicative Uncertainty

Multiplicative uncertainty is a simple and convenient model to characterize plant uncertainty. Since it can take into account not only unmodeled dynamics but also some effect of parametric uncertainty, a low dimensional Δ is therefore adequate for the design purpose. In the dual-stage actuator, two multiplicative uncertainties are assumed for the VCM and MA respectively:

$$\begin{aligned} G_V(s) &= G_{V\text{nom}}(s)(1 + \Delta_V(s)W_V(s)), \\ G_M(s) &= G_{M\text{nom}}(s)(1 + \Delta_M(s)W_M(s)), \end{aligned} \tag{2.8}$$

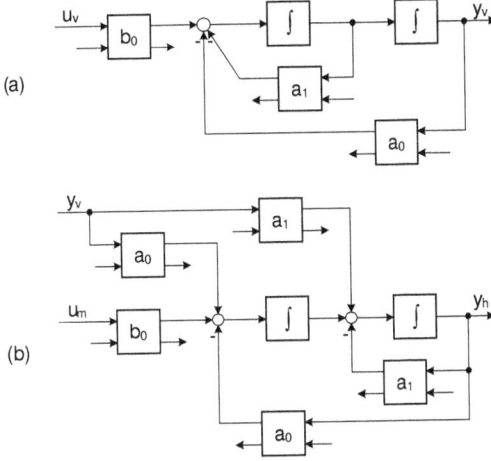

Figure 2.5: Representation of parametric uncertainties with repeatedness (a) for each VCM/suspension mode and the rotational MA mode (b) for the translational MA combining G_M and G_C

where $G_{V\mathrm{nom}}$ and $G_{M\mathrm{nom}}$ are the nominal dynamics of the VCM and MA respectively, $||\Delta_V||_\infty \leq 1$, $||\Delta_M||_\infty \leq 1$, and W_V and W_M are the magnitude bounding functions for the two uncertainties:

$$W_V(s) = 0.6\frac{s + 2\pi \times 400}{s + 2\pi \times 6000},$$
$$W_M(s) = 0.3\frac{s + 2\pi \times 1400}{s + 2\pi \times 10000}. \tag{2.9}$$

2.3.3 A Mathematical Expression of Plant Uncertainties

Combining all those uncertainties defined above, we can obtain a mathematical expression for the set of perturbation matrices

$$\Delta = \left\{ \begin{array}{l} \mathrm{diag}\left[\delta_{V_1}, \ldots, \delta_{V_p}, \delta_{M_1}, \delta_{M_2}I_{M_2}, \delta_{M_3}I_{M_3}, \Delta_{dv}, \Delta_{dm}\right] : \\ \delta_{V_i} \in \mathbb{R}, \ \delta_{M_j} \in \mathbb{R}, \\ \Delta_{dv} \in \mathbb{C}, \ \Delta_{dm} \in \mathbb{C}, \end{array} \right\}, \tag{2.10}$$

where $\delta_{V_1}, \ldots, \delta_{V_p}$ are the parametric uncertainties of the VCM, $\delta_{M_1}, \delta_{M_2}, \delta_{M_3}$ are the real parametric uncertainties of the MA, Δ_{dv} and Δ_{dm} are the dynamic multiplicative uncertainties of the VCM and MA respectively. If the MA is rotational, then I_{M_2} and I_{M_3} are just of dimension one. On the other hand, if the MA is translational, then due to the coupling between G_C and G_M, the parametric uncertainties of ω_m and ζ_m are repeated twice, and hence I_{M_2} and I_{M_3} are 2-by-2 identity matrices. When all uncertainties are

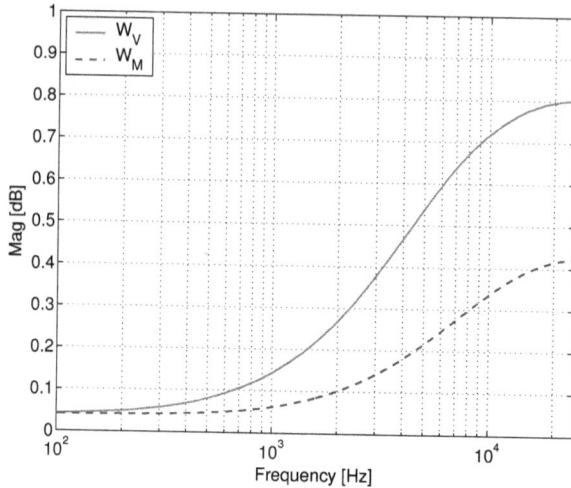

Figure 2.6: Multiplicative uncertainties

normalized, and all gains and weighting dynamics, such as $W_V(s)$ and $W_M(s)$, have been incorporated into the generalized plant, we have the unity norm bounded subset of $\mathbf{\Delta}$,

$$\mathbf{B_\Delta} = \{\Delta \in \mathbf{\Delta} \; : \; \bar{\sigma}(\Delta) \le 1\} . \tag{2.11}$$

2.4 Multirate Sensing and Multirate Control

In conventional single-stage disk drives, the only feedback signal, PES:$= r - y_h$, has a fixed sampling rate that is predetermined by the disk rotation speed and the number of servo sectors per track. For example, a 7200-RPM disk drive with 180 servo sectors has a PES sampling frequency of 21.6 kHz. Given the disk rotation speed, a higher PES sampling frequency requires more servo sectors and reduces storage efficiency. This fixed sampling frequency limits the expected servo bandwidth which is about one tenth of this frequency. Further increase of servo bandwidth is also prevented by the presence of suspension resonance modes. The open-loop crossover frequency should be far away from the major suspension modes so that sufficient gain and phase margins are retained to accommodate variations of these modes.

For a designed servo system, all disturbances with frequencies below the closed-loop bandwidth can be attenuated to some extent. However, high frequency disturbances, especially those excited by airflow turbulence, will be amplified, according to the theorem of Bode's integral equality. As a result, airflow excited suspension vibration has become a major obstacle to achieving the targeted track density of 500,000 TPI, which requires a track TMR budget of less than 5 nm (3σ). However, with strain sensors instrumented on the suspension and with a secondary actuator, high frequency suspension vibrations may be effectively suppressed and compensated by feeding the vibration information to the controller [37]. Furthermore, the sampling rate of the two signals can be higher than that of the PES for better performance. In some design schemes, the VCM and MA are intended to deal with the attenuation of low frequency and high frequency disturbances respectively, then u_v can be updated at a lower rate than that of u_m for computation saving [62]. A multirate sensing scheme is carried out and a multirate controller can then be designed accordingly.

In order to mathematically express the multirate sampler S and the multirate hold H, the original continuous-time linear time-invariant (LTI) plant is first discretized at the fastest rate f_f with the shortest period T_f. It is assumed that all periods of the sampler S and the hold H are integer multiples of T_f. Then we know that all periods of the multi-channel sampler are rationally related, that is, their least common multiple

$$T_s := \text{l.c.m.}(T_{si}), \quad i = 1, 2, \ldots, n_y, \tag{2.12}$$

is an integer multiple of T_f, where n_y is the dimension of the sampler S. It is also noted that all periods of the multi-channel hold are rationally related, that is,

$$T_h := \text{l.c.m.}(T_{hi}), \quad i = 1, 2, \ldots, n_u, \tag{2.13}$$

is an integer multiple of T_f, where n_u is the dimension of the hold H. It is further noted that the periods T_s and T_h are rationally related, that is,

$$T_p := \text{l.c.m.}(T_s, T_h) \tag{2.14}$$

is also an integer multiple of T_f. Obviously, T_p is the period of the overall plant which already includes the sampler S and hold H.

Now the multirate sampler S can be expressed mathematically as

$$S : \tilde{y}(k) = \Gamma(k)y(k), \quad k = 0, 1, 2, \ldots, \tag{2.15}$$

where $\tilde{y}(k)$ is the actually measured plant output and $\Gamma(k)$ is a diagonal matrix with entries of 1 or 0. If the i-th output channel is measured at time k, then the (i,i)-entry of $\Gamma(k)$ is set to 1; otherwise it is set to 0. In the single-rate case, $\Gamma(k) = I$ for all $k = 0, 1, 2, \ldots$. By assumption,

$$\Gamma(k + T_s) = \Gamma(k), \quad k = 0, 1, 2, \ldots. \tag{2.16}$$

To represent the multirate hold H mathematically, we decompose the plant input vector u into two vectors with the fastest rate and other slower hold rates as follows

$$u = \begin{bmatrix} u_s \\ u_f \end{bmatrix}, \tag{2.17}$$

where the dimensions of u_s and u_f are n_{us} and n_{uf} respectively. u_s includes all channels that have slower rates than f_f, and u_f includes all channels that have the fastest rate f_f, implying that all elements in u_f are updated at every time k. Then, the hold is a mapping

$$H : \tilde{u} = \begin{bmatrix} \tilde{u}_s \\ \tilde{u}_f \end{bmatrix} \rightarrow \begin{bmatrix} u_s \\ u_f \end{bmatrix}, \tag{2.18}$$

where $\tilde{u}$ is the output from the controller to the hold, and u is the output from the hold to the plant. This mapping can be described as a dynamic linear time-varying (LTV) system

$$\begin{bmatrix} x_h(k+1) \\ \begin{bmatrix} u_s(k) \\ u_f(k) \end{bmatrix} \end{bmatrix} = \begin{bmatrix} A_h(k) & B_h(k) \\ C_h(k) & D_h(k) \end{bmatrix} \begin{bmatrix} x_h(k) \\ \begin{bmatrix} \tilde{u}_s(k) \\ \tilde{u}_f(k) \end{bmatrix} \end{bmatrix}, \tag{2.19}$$

where x_h is the state vector of H, and for $k = 0, 1, 2, \ldots$,

$$\begin{aligned} A_h(k) &:= I_{n_{ss}} - \Omega(k), & B_h(k) &:= [\Omega(k) \ 0], \\ C_h(k) &:= \begin{bmatrix} I_{n_{ss}} - \Omega(k) \\ 0 \end{bmatrix}, & D_h(k) &:= \begin{bmatrix} \Omega(k) & 0 \\ 0 & I_{n_{sf}} \end{bmatrix}. \end{aligned} \tag{2.20}$$

Here, $\Omega(k) \in \mathbb{R}^{n_{us} \times n_{us}}$ is a diagonal matrix with diagonal entries of 0 or 1, and plays a similar role to $\Gamma(k)$. If we feed the i-th input signal of $\tilde{u}_s$ from the controller to the hold at time k, then the (i, i)-entry of $\Omega(k)$ is set to 1; otherwise, it is set to 0, resulting in the i-th input at time k that is equal to the i-th input at step $k - 1$. In the single-rate case, the hold reduces to a static system $u(k) = \tilde{u}(k)$ with $n_{us} = 0$ and $n_{uf} = n_u$. Also by assumption, the hold is periodic with the period T_h, i.e.,

$$\Omega(k + T_h) = \Omega(k), \quad k = 0, 1, 2, \ldots. \tag{2.21}$$

In this paper, the PES is measured at 25 kHz, and both y_p and y_m are sampled at 50 kHz. For simplicity, both u_v and u_m are updated at the high rate of 50 kHz. Then the multirate sampler has a period of $2T_f$, and the single-rate hold has a period of T_f with $u = u_f$.

2.5 A Generalized Plant with Multirate Sensing and Multirate Control

Combining all of those models for disturbances, measurement noises, and uncertainties in the previous sections, we can obtain a complete plant with both multirate sensing and multirate control, as shown in Fig. 2.7. This system can be simplified to a standard representation as shown in Fig. 2.8. In that figure, Δ represents all types of normalized perturbations in block-diagonal form. $w_2 := [w_r \ w_v\{6\} \ w_r \ n\{3\}]^T$ includes all types of normalized white disturbances. $z_2 := [\text{PES} \ u_v \ u_m]^T$ is the weighted performance output. The weights on u_v and u_m are taken to be the reciprocals of their corresponding upper bounds, which are both 2 volts multiplied by the corresponding amplification gains of their conditioning circuits. S is the multirate sampler of the plant measurement output $y := [\text{PES} \ y_p \ y_m]^T$, and H is the multirate zero order hold of the control input $u := [u_v \ u_m]^T$. $\tilde{y}$ and $\tilde{u}$ are the actual input and output of the multirate controller K.

When discretized at the fastest rate f_f, the discrete-time LTI generalized plant with an uncertainty block can be expressed as

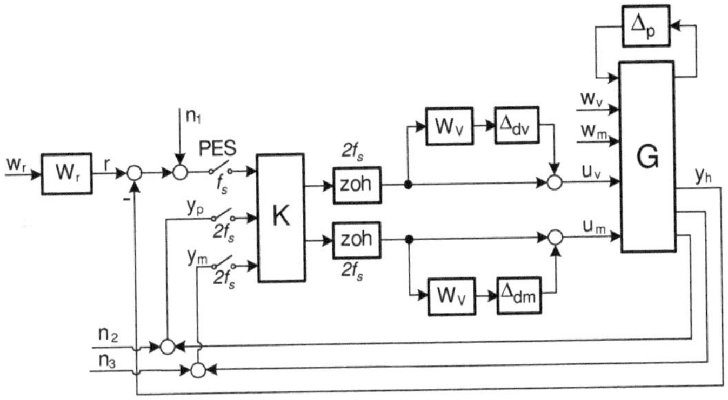

Figure 2.7: The complete plant model

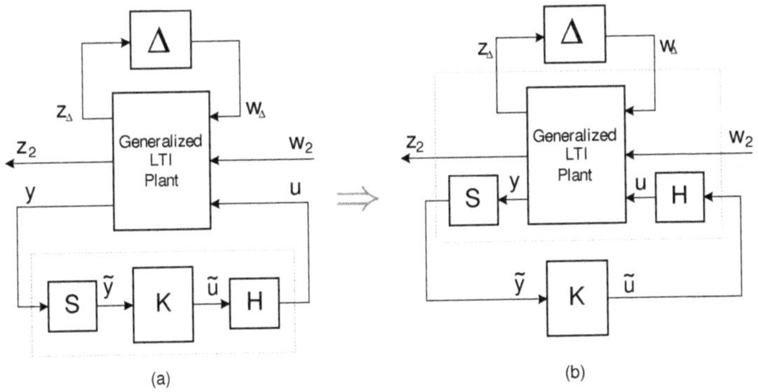

Figure 2.8: (a) The LTI plant with an uncertainty block Δ and a multirate controller HKS
(b) The periodically time-varying system with an uncertainty block Δ and a controller K

$$
\begin{bmatrix} z_\Delta \\ z_2 \\ y \end{bmatrix} = \left[\begin{array}{c|ccc} A & B_\Delta & B_2 & B_u \\ \hline C_\Delta & D_{\Delta\Delta} & D_{\Delta 2} & D_{\Delta u} \\ C_2 & D_{2\Delta} & D_{22} & D_{2u} \\ C_y & D_{y\Delta} & D_{y2} & 0 \end{array} \right] \begin{bmatrix} w_\Delta \\ w_2 \\ u \end{bmatrix},
\tag{2.22}
$$

where we have used the standard notation:

$$
\left[\begin{array}{c|c} A & B \\ \hline C & D \end{array} \right] := D + C(zI - A)^{-1}B.
\tag{2.23}
$$

Then, by combining (2.22), (2.15) and (2.19), we obtain the linear periodically time-varying system with the period T_p, as shown in Fig. 2.8(b):

$$
\begin{bmatrix} \tilde{x}(k+1) \\ z_\Delta(k) \\ z_2(k) \\ \tilde{y}(k) \end{bmatrix} = \begin{bmatrix} \tilde{A}(k) & \tilde{B}_\Delta(k) & \tilde{B}_2(k) & \tilde{B}_u(k) \\ \tilde{C}_\Delta(k) & \tilde{D}_{\Delta\Delta}(k) & \tilde{D}_{\Delta2}(k) & \tilde{D}_{\Delta u}(k) \\ \tilde{C}_2(k) & \tilde{D}_{2\Delta}(k) & \tilde{D}_{22}(k) & \tilde{D}_{2u}(k) \\ \tilde{C}_y(k) & \tilde{D}_{y\Delta}(k) & \tilde{D}_{y2}(k) & 0 \end{bmatrix} \begin{bmatrix} \tilde{x}(k) \\ w_\Delta(k) \\ w_2(k) \\ \tilde{u}(k) \end{bmatrix} \tag{2.24}
$$

for $k = 0, 1, 2, \ldots$, where the matrices in (2.24) are obtained by straightforward calculation as

$$
\tilde{A}(k) = \begin{bmatrix} A & B_u C_h(k) \\ 0 & A_h(k) \end{bmatrix}, \quad \tilde{B}_\Delta(k) = \begin{bmatrix} B_\Delta \\ 0 \end{bmatrix}, \quad \tilde{B}_2(k) = \begin{bmatrix} B_2 \\ 0 \end{bmatrix}, \quad \tilde{B}_u(k) = \begin{bmatrix} B_u D_h(k) \\ B_h(k) \end{bmatrix},
$$

$$
\tilde{C}_\Delta(k) = \begin{bmatrix} C_\Delta & D_{\Delta u} C_h(k) \end{bmatrix}, \quad \tilde{D}_{\Delta\Delta}(k) = D_{\Delta\Delta}, \quad \tilde{D}_{\Delta2}(k) = D_{\Delta2}, \quad \tilde{D}_{\Delta u}(k) = D_{\Delta u} D_h(k),
$$

$$
\tilde{C}_2(k) = \begin{bmatrix} C_2 & D_{2u} C_h(k) \end{bmatrix}, \quad \tilde{D}_{2\Delta}(k) = D_{2\Delta}, \quad \tilde{D}_{22}(k) = D_{22}, \quad \tilde{D}_{2u}(k) = D_{2u} D_h(k),
$$

$$
\tilde{C}_y(k) = \Gamma(k) \begin{bmatrix} C_y & 0 \end{bmatrix}, \quad \tilde{D}_{y\Delta}(k) = \Gamma(k) D_{y\Delta}, \quad \tilde{D}_{y2}(k) = \Gamma(k) D_{y2}.
$$

Note that the system (2.24) has incorporated all the information about the multirate sampler and hold.

The generalized plant has absorbed all frequency shaping filters and weights, in order to normalize those perturbations, disturbances, and performance outputs. Based on this generalized model, various design approaches, either SISO or MIMO, can be applied to design the controller K.

Chapter 3

Track-Following Controller Design of the Dual-Stage System Using SISO Design Approaches

This chapter discusses the track-following control design of the dual-stage system, either rotational or translational, using SISO design approaches. There have been several SISO design approaches applied to disk drive dual-stage servos, such as the SD method, the PQ method, the master-slave method, etc. All of them first decompose the original MIMO plant into serial or cascaded SISO loops, to which classic SISO design techniques, such as frequency shaping and pole placement, can be applied. When y_p and y_m are available as auxiliary information, it is possible to first design some minor loop vibration damping controllers before designing outer loop tracking controllers. Compared to MIMO design approaches, SISO design ones are straightforward to implement and are more tractable. We usually know how to design sub-loop controllers individually, and much empirical knowledge can be utilized during the design process. However, since the coupling property of the MIMO plant has not been fully exploited during SISO design, the resulting performance is usually not so good as that of a system designed by MIMO design approaches.

3.1 Minor Loop Design of Vibration Damping and Compensation

As mentioned before, the two signals, y_p and y_m, can be sampled at a higher rate than that of the PES, low frequency inner loops can be designed in order to achieve better control performance. Fig. 3.1 shows the minor loop control structure, in which G_p is the dual-stage plant as shown in Fig. 2.2 and has been discretized at the highest rate of 50 kHz. It is noted that the MA in the dual-stage plant can be either rotational or translational. The difference between the two configurations will be analyzed in detail later.

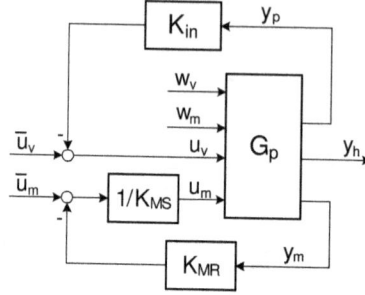

Figure 3.1: Minor loop vibration damping and compensation

3.1.1 Microactuator Damping Using y_m

The basic use of the relative motion signal, y_m, is to actively damp the microactuator resonance mode to make for a well-behaved MA and to simplify the control design that follows. When the MA is lightly damped, variation of its natural frequency and damping ratio can greatly affect the system stability and performance, since its natural frequency is close to the closed-loop servo bandwidth. MA damping can be implemented by a minor loop around the MA as shown in the lower part of Fig. 3.1. To begin with, we express the transfer function from u_m to y_h and y_m as

$$G_M(q^{-1}) = \frac{q^{-1}B_o(q^{-1})}{A_o(q^{-1})}, \tag{3.1}$$

where q^{-1} is the one-step delay operator, $B_o(q^{-1})$ and $A_o(q^{-1})$ are the plant zero and pole polynomials, respectively. The desired damped MA can be expressed as

$$G_{MD}(q^{-1}) = \frac{q^{-1}B_o(q^{-1})}{A_D(q^{-1})}, \tag{3.2}$$

where $A_D(q^{-1})$ is the desired characteristic polynomial. Usually $A_D(q^{-1})$ is chosen such that the MA damping coefficient is about 1, and its poles, or equivalently ω_{md}, may also be set at desired locations. With the compensator structure shown in the lower part of Fig. 3.1, we can get the closed-loop transfer function for the MA

$$G_{MD}(q^{-1}) = \frac{q^{-1}B_o(q^{-1})}{A_o(q^{-1})K_{MS}(q^{-1}) + B_o(q^{-1})K_{MR}(q^{-1})}. \tag{3.3}$$

Equating (3.2) with (3.3) yields the following Diophantine equation

$$A_D(q^{-1}) = A_o(q^{-1})K_{MS}(q^{-1}) + q^{-1}B_o(q^{-1})K_{MR}(q^{-1}). \tag{3.4}$$

The desired compensators, K_{MS} and K_{MR}, are then obtained by solving the above Diophantine equation.

3.1.2   Suspension Damping Using y_p

After the minor loop compensator is closed around the MA, a vibration controller K_{in} can be designed using y_p to provide more damping of some of the suspension resonance modes [28][37]. The design of K_{in} is formulated as a standard LQG problem. Consider the discrete-time representation of the plant with the MA damped by K_{MS} and K_{MR}

$$x(k+1) = Ax(k) + Bu_v(k) + B_w w_v(k),$$
$$y(k) = Cx(k) + n(k),$$
(3.5)

where $y(k) = [y_h(k)\ y_p(k)]^T$, and $n(k) = [n_h(k)\ n_p(k)]^T$ are the measurement noises. For the design purpose, only two major suspension modes at 7.4 kHz and 10.7 kHz are considered in order to restrain the designed controller order. The goal of designing K_{in} is to minimize the cost function

$$J := E\left\{y_h^2(k) + Ru_v^2(k)\right\},$$
(3.6)

where $E\{\cdot\}$ is the expectation operator and R is the weighting on control input u_v.

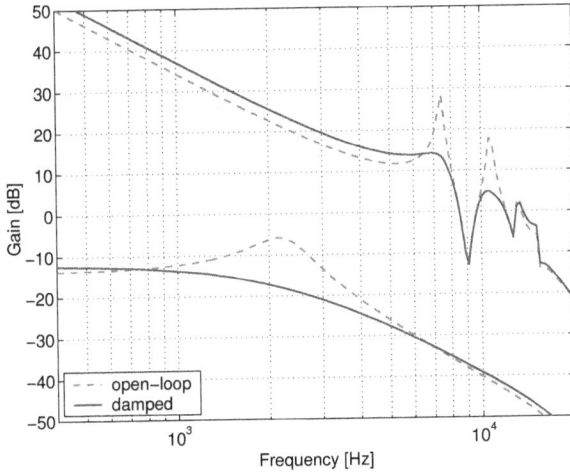

Figure 3.2: Frequency responses of G_V and G_M (rotational MA)

Fig. 3.2 shows the damping effect of the rotational dual-stage plant. Two major resonance modes of the VCM and the MA mode are damped by using y_p and y_m, respectively. The damping effect not only improves the robustness to mode variation but also suppresses airflow excited suspension and MA vibration. Fig. 3.3 compares the filtering effect between the rotational and translational plants with damping. As can be seen, the frequency response of G_H for the translational MA case has stronger attenuation in the high frequency range than that for the rotational MA case due to the coupling-filtering effect as shown in Fig. 2.4. This implies that the translational MA will behave better in suspension vibration attenuation which mainly happens in the high frequency range.

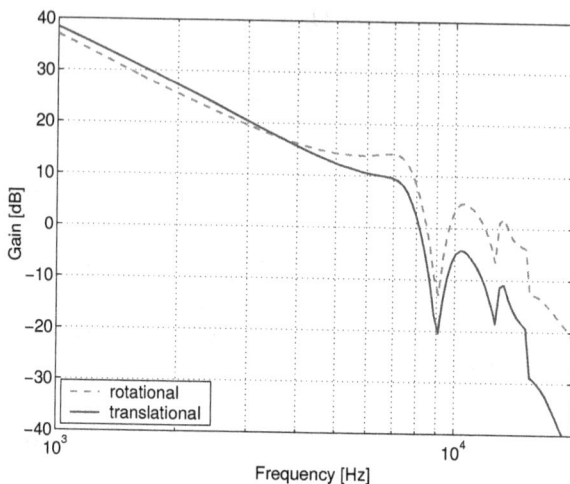

Figure 3.3: Frequency responses of G_H of the dual-stage plant after damping

3.2 Outer Loop Servo Design Using the SD Design Method

As mentioned before, the strain sensor output y_p and the relative motion of the MA y_m are sampled at 50 kHz. But the PES is available at 25 kHz due to hardware limitations. Thus the fast-rate damped plant needs to be down-sampled by a factor of 2 in order to accommodate the sampling rate of the PES and to design low-rate outer loop compensators.

The SD design method, originally introduced by [40], has been popularly applied to the design of track-following controllers for dual-stage servo systems with a rotational MA [34]. This approach utilizes the PES and y_m to generate the position error signal of the suspension tip relative to the data track center, which is also called the VCM PES, or simply VPES:

$$VPES = PES + y_m = r - y_v. \qquad (3.7)$$

From the variable name, it is clear that this information is fed to the VCM loop and should be compensated by the VCM controller K_V. With this configuration as shown in Fig. 3.4(a), the decoupling design of K_V and K_M is made clear: the VCM loop and the MA loop can be designed sequentially using conventional SISO design techniques such as pole placement.

It is worthwhile to pay special attention to the coupling effect in this design process. The blocks G_{C1} and G_{C2} in Fig. 3.4 are derived from the coupling effect G_C as shown in

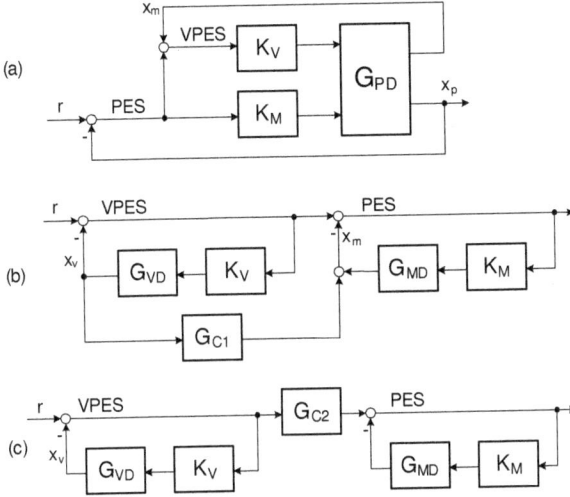

Figure 3.4: Block diagram of the sensitivity decoupling design method

Fig. 2.2 and (2.3):

$$G_{C1} = \frac{K_{MS}}{K_{MS} + G_M K_{MR}}(G_C - 1), \tag{3.8}$$

$$G_{C2} = 1 - G_{C1} G_V K_V. \tag{3.9}$$

As can be seen, for a rotational MA, $G_C = 1$, then $G_{C1} = 0$ and $G_{C2} = 1$, implying complete decoupling between the two minor loops in Fig. 3.4(c). In the translational MA case, G_{C2} involves all plant dynamics and controllers designed except for K_M. The frequency response of G_{C2} is shown in Fig. 3.5. It is seen that the frequency response of G_{C2} is fairly mild: it is about 6 dB in the region of 60~500 Hz, and close to zero dB beyond 1 kHz. Its phase property is mild as well: 30 degrees around 60 Hz and -30 degrees around 600 Hz. This implies that based on the K_M designed for the rotational MA case, a modifier which has the similar dynamics to G_{C2} can be designed to compensate for the coupling effect, yielding a sensitivity response similar to that of the rotational MA case:

$$K_{MC} = K_M K_C \approx K_M G_{C2}, \tag{3.10}$$

where K_M is the servo controller designed for the rotational MA case, K_C is the modifier to cancel the effect of G_{C2}, and its dynamics are also shown in Fig. 3.5 by dashed lines.

In the rotational MA case, pole placement is applied to design K_V and K_M. First, the VCM loop compensator, K_V, is designed to attain a desired VCM loop sensitivity, S_V, as shown in Fig. 3.6. Its bandwidth is generally limited by the arm and suspension resonance modes. As mentioned in the previous section, the MA mode has been adequately damped by using the relative position signal y_m. Also, the MA's low frequency gain can

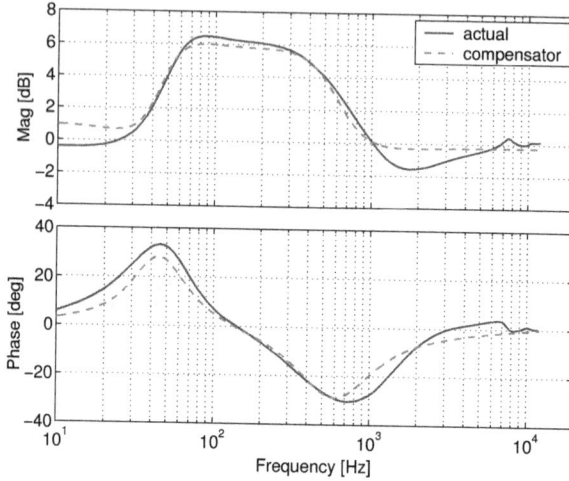

Figure 3.5: Frequency responses of G_{C2} and the compensator K_C

be increased by shifting its resonance frequency, ω_{md}, to a low frequency. Then the PES loop compensator, K_M, is designed to place the poles of the MA closed-loop sensitivity S_M, as shown in Fig. 3.6. Its bandwidth is mainly limited by the PES sampling frequency and computational delay. The total dual-stage sensitivity is then the product of the two sub-sensitivities,

$$S_{\mathrm{cl}} = S_V S_M . \tag{3.11}$$

In this design example, K_V is designed to achieve a closed-loop bandwidth of 600 Hz for the VCM loop, and K_M achieves a closed-loop bandwidth of 3 kHz for the MA loop. The final sensitivity is the product of the two, and it achieves a closed-loop bandwidth of 2.4 kHz. Their frequency responses are shown in Fig. 3.6, and the comparison between the designs for rotational and translational MAs is shown in Fig. 3.7. From that figure we see that, after inserting a modifier K_C into the MA loop, the translational system achieves almost the same sensitivity response as the rotational one.

For the purpose of comparison with other design approaches, the structure of the complete multirate controller designed by sensitivity decoupling, K_{SD}, can be derived by plugging Fig. 3.1 in Fig. 3.4(a) and becomes

$$K_{SD} = \begin{bmatrix} K_V & -K_{\mathrm{in}} & K_V \\ K_{MS}K_M & 0 & -K_{MS}K_{MR} \end{bmatrix} \tag{3.12}$$

with input $[\text{PES } y_p \, y_m]^T$ and output $[u_v \, u_m]^T$. From this expression we can clearly see the constraints imposed on the controller structure for the ease of implementing sensitivity decoupling. The second column is determined by the inner loop vibration damping using y_p, and the other two columns are determined by the outer loop controller and MA damping. The zero value of the (2,2)-entry implies that y_p has not been utilized by the

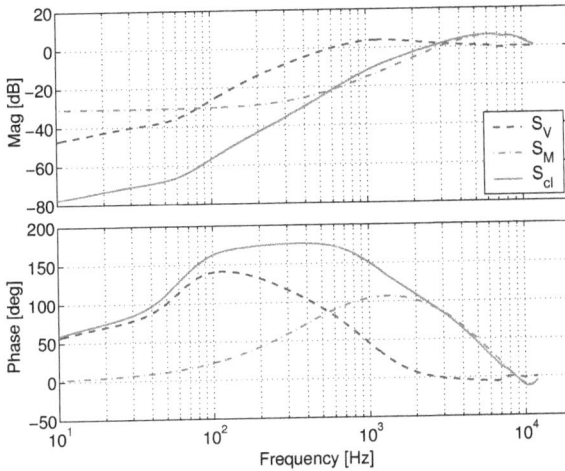

Figure 3.6: Sensitivities of the decoupling design with a rotational MA

MA. Instead, adaptive feedforward control will be applied in real time to alleviate this limitation.

3.3   Outer Loop Servo Design Using the PQ Design Method

The second SISO design approach is called the PQ method [51], which reduces a controller design problem for dual-input single-output (DISO) systems to two standard controller design problems for SISO systems. The first part of the PQ method directly addresses the issue of actuator output contribution as a function of frequency, and the second part allows the use of traditional loop shaping techniques to achieve the final performance. Its schematic structure is shown in Fig. 3.8, in which the plant is already closed by the MA damping controller, K_{MS} and K_{MR}, and the vibration damping and compensation controller K_{in}. By definitions (2.4) and (2.2), G_1 and G_2 can be replaced by G_H and G_M respectively. We will use the translational dual-stage plant to demonstrate how the PQ method is applied.

To begin with, let us first define

$$G_P(z) := \frac{G_1(z)}{G_2(z)}, \tag{3.13}$$

which is just the ratio between the two input-output channels of the plant as shown in Fig. 3.8. Then design a compensator

$$G_Q(z) := \frac{K_1(z)}{K_2(z)} \tag{3.14}$$

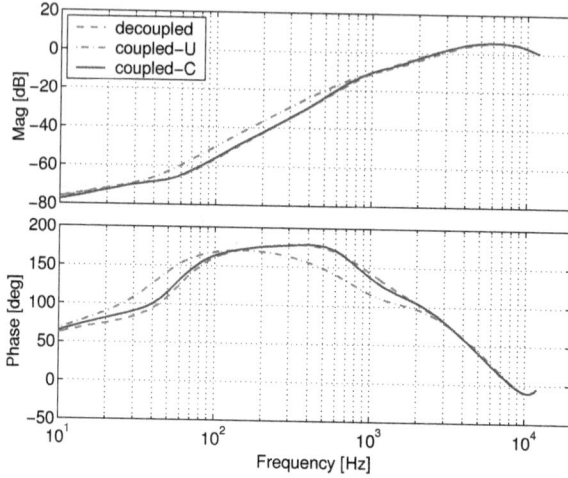

Figure 3.7: Comparison of sensitivities for rotational and translational MAs. "decoupled": original design for the rotational MA case; "coupled-U": the same controllers applied to the translational MA case without compensation by K_C; "coupled-C": the system is compensated by K_C.

to stabilize the virtual plant $G_P(z)$. The virtual open-loop transfer function, $G_{PQ} := G_P G_Q$, is essentially the ratio between the two actuator contributions to y_h with the same input. A typical frequency response is shown in Fig. 3.9 with solid lines. In the low frequency range, its magnitude is much higher than 0 dB, meaning that the VCM dominates the head motion. In the high frequency range below 0 dB, the MA dominates the head motion. When the magnitude is close to 0 dB, we want the two actuators to work cooperatively, that is, the phase difference between them, or equivalently the phase of G_{PQ}, should be far away from -180° in order to avoid cancelling each other completely. The difference between the phase of G_{PQ} at 0 dB and -180° is exactly defined by the phase margin of the virtual system G_{PQ} with unity negative feedback. A large phase margin is desired to ensure that the two outputs combine constructively around the handoff frequency region. The designed G_Q is then decomposed into two parts with $G_Q(z) = K_1(z)/K_2(z)$, such that both $K_1(z)$ and $K_2(z)$ are realizable.

Here, loop shaping techniques are used in designing G_Q. The final G_Q includes a PI controller with the break frequency at 100 Hz to ensure zero steady-state error, and a complex-valued lead compensator with a phase peak of 20° at 1.4 kHz.

$$G_Q(z) = K_{\mathrm{PI}}(z) K_{\mathrm{lead1}}(z). \tag{3.15}$$

The virtual feedback system G_{PQ} has the phase margin of 56°. The frequency response of G_{PQ} is shown in Fig. 3.9. Since $G_Q(z)$ is already realizable, it is straightforward to let $K_2(z) = 1$ and $K_1(z) = G_Q(z)$.

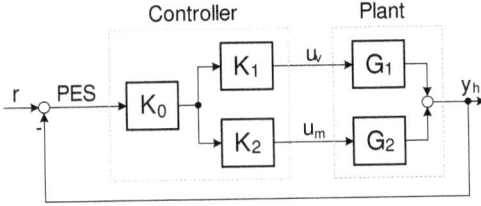

Figure 3.8: Block diagram for the PQ design method

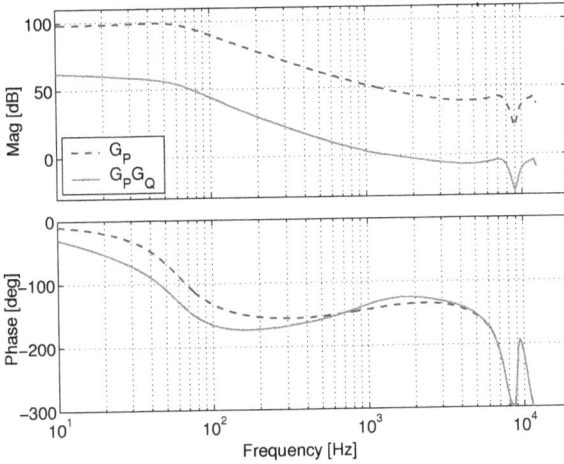

Figure 3.9: Frequency responses of G_P and G_{PQ}

With K_1 and K_2 connected to G_1 and G_2 respectively, a compensator K_0 can be designed for the SISO plant

$$G_{\text{siso}} := K_1 G_1 + K_2 G_2 . \qquad (3.16)$$

This is again fulfilled by using loop shaping techniques. K_0 is designed to be a combination of a lag compensator K_{lag} for better error rejection in the low frequency range, a lead compensator K_{lead2} for adequate phase margin around the crossover frequency, and a notch filter K_{notch} for high frequency peak suppression.

$$K_0(z) = K_{\text{lag}}(z) K_{\text{lead2}}(z) K_{\text{notch}}(z) . \qquad (3.17)$$

The open-loop frequency response of $G_{\text{siso}} K_0$ is shown in Fig. 3.10. The closed-loop system achieves the gain margin of 7.56 dB and the phase margin of 35.3°. The frequency response of the sensitivity transfer function is shown in Fig. 3.11.

As in the sensitivity decoupling design, the complete controller, K_{PQ}, of the PQ

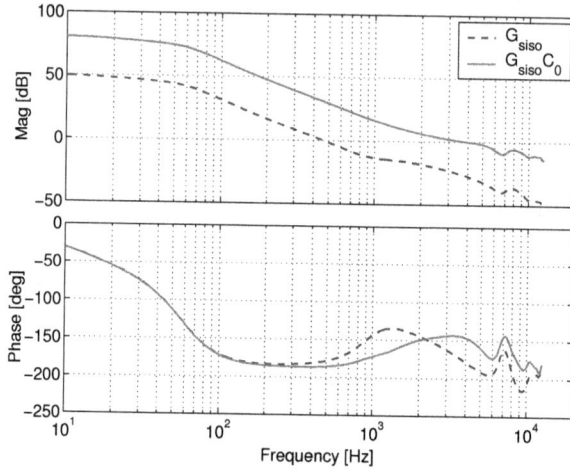

Figure 3.10: Frequency responses of G_{siso} and $G_{\text{siso}}K_0$

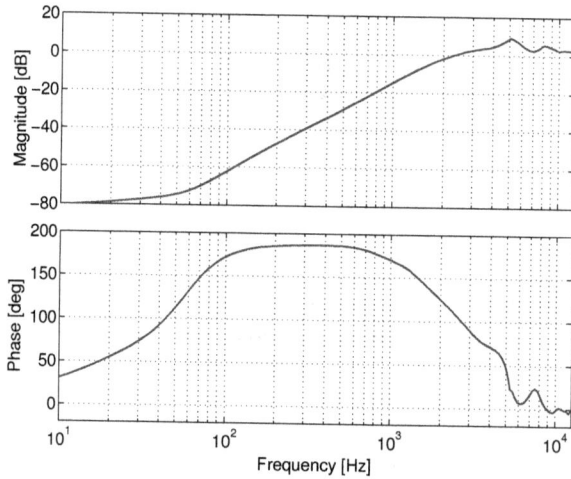

Figure 3.11: Bode plot of sensitivity function designed by the PQ method

design can be derived to be

$$K_{PQ} = \begin{bmatrix} K_1 K_0 & -K_{in} & 0 \\ K_{MS} K_2 K_0 & 0 & -K_{MS} K_{MR} \end{bmatrix}. \tag{3.18}$$

Unlike the sensitivity decoupling design, the PQ design uses only the PES for designing the outer loop tracking controller. Therefore, the structure of K_{PQ} is more constrained than that of K_{SD} in that, besides the (2,1)-entry, the (1,3)-entry is also zero.

3.4 Adaptive Feedforward Compensation for Suspension Vibration

As mentioned before, some suspension resonance modes can be damped by using the strain sensor signal y_p measured from the suspension surface. Actually this signal can further be exploited to drive the MA to compensate for the airflow excited suspension vibrations appearing at y_h [33][25].

Define G_{wp} and G_{wh} to be the transfer functions from w_v to y_p and y_h, respectively. We want the feedforward compensator, K_{MF}, to minimize the airflow excited vibrations at the head, i.e., to minimize

$$e_w = G_M K_{MF} G_{wp} w_v + G_{wh} w_v . \tag{3.19}$$

This mechanism is different from the feedback damping of the VCM in that, the motion generated by the MA cannot directly affect the suspension outputs, y_v and y_p. Therefore, what it can do is to *compensate* for the vibrations at the head that result from suspension vibrations. This assumption has been made during system modeling and will be validated experimentally.

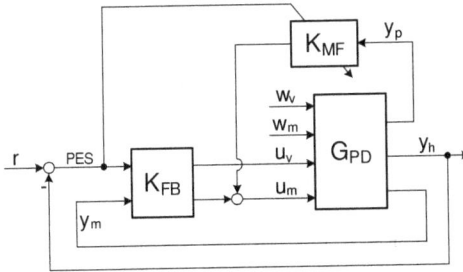

Figure 3.12: Block diagram of adaptive feedforward compensation

Although K_{MF} can be designed to have fixed coefficients, it is desirable to tune the coefficients of K_{MF} in real time in order to take into account the following time-varying factors: suspension dynamics vary slightly from drive to drive; the characteristics of airflow turbulence vary with radial track position; strain sensor properties may be sensitive to ambient temperature and may even change with time due to aging, etc. In this design, K_{MF} assumes the form of finite impulse response (FIR) for stability consideration, that is, the compensator itself is always stable no matter how its coefficients are tuned.

$$K_{MF}(\theta, q^{-1}) = h_0 + h_1 q^{-1} + \cdots + h_n q^{-n}, \tag{3.20}$$

where θ is the filter coefficient vector $\theta = [h_0 \, h_1 \cdots h_n]^T$ and n is the order of K_{MF}. The feedforward compensation motion can be expressed as

$$\begin{aligned} y_{MF}(k) &= G_M(q^{-1}) K_{MF}(q^{-1}) y_p(k) \\ &= K_{MF}(q^{-1}) G_M(q^{-1}) y_p(k) \\ &= K_{MF}(q^{-1}) x_f(k) \\ &= \theta^T \phi(k-1), \end{aligned} \tag{3.21}$$

where $x_f(k) = G_M(q^{-1}) y_p(k)$, and $\phi(k) = [x_f(k) \, x_f(k-1) \cdots x_f(k-n)]^T$. Since $x_f(k)$ is not directly measurable, it is estimated by passing $y_p(k)$ through the model of the MA, $\hat{G}_M$:

$$x_f(k) = \hat{G}_M(q^{-1}) y_p(k). \tag{3.22}$$

The coefficients of θ are tuned in such a way that $E\{e_w^2(k)\}$ is minimized. However, e_w is not directly measurable, what we have is the PES, and it can be written as

$$\text{PES}(k) = e_w(k) + e_r(k), \tag{3.23}$$

where e_r represents the tracking error resulting from all other disturbance sources except the airflow turbulence acting on the VCM-suspension assembly. It is roughly valid to assume that w_v and r are uncorrelated, then we have

$$E\{\text{PES}^2(k)\} = E\{e_v^2(k)\} + E\{e_r^2(k)\}. \tag{3.24}$$

Thus, minimizing $E\{e_v^2(k)\}$ is equivalent to minimizing $E\{\text{PES}^2(k)\}$, and we can use the PES as a corrupted compensation error signal to perform the adaptation of θ. With e_v corrupted by e_r, there will be some degradation in feedforward compensation performance, and a little longer time is expected for the adaptation process to converge.

It is noted that, adaptive feedforward compensation does not affect the stability of the already designed and closed feedback system, since it is an add-on part and aims at minimizing the RMS value of the PES by generating additional motion at the MA to compensate for it. Therefore, the vibration compensation part can be implemented on any already-stabilized closed-loop system, no matter the plant has a rotational or translational MA, or what kind of feedback controller is used. It is also expected that feedforward compensation will be more useful in the rotational MA case than in the translational one, since in the rotational MA case, suspension vibration at y_v will equally show up at y_h without any mechanical attenuation. These observations will be verified by the simulation results in Chapter 5.

Chapter 4

Track-Following Controller Design of the Dual-Stage System Using MIMO Design Approaches

This chapter discusses the design of dual-stage track-following controllers using MIMO design approaches. Compared to SISO design approaches, MIMO design approaches inherently account for the coupling dynamics of the dual-stage plant and can expectedly achieve better performance. Furthermore, stability robustness can be explicitly considered during the design process by imposing some H_∞ norm or even μ bounds. The information about plant uncertainty type and perturbation range is therefore necessary for constructing a realistic uncertainty model. In this chapter, three multi-objective optimization methods are discussed: mixed H_2/H_∞, mixed H_2/μ, and robust H_2. In the first two methods, the nominal performance and stability robustness are considered simultaneously, while in the last method, performance robustness is considered, in which robust stability is guaranteed implicitly. These methods formulate multiple objectives as a problem of some norm optimization or norm constraints that can be expressed as a set of linear matrix inequalities (LMIs), to which there are numerically efficient algorithms and software available [56][10].

4.1   Mixed H_2/H_∞ Synthesis

In this section, mixed H_2/H_∞ synthesis is discussed, which simultaneously considers H_2 performance optimization and robust stability by H_∞ norm bounds. In the context of disk drive servo design, this design approach was first applied in [54] to a single-stage disk drive servo system. The design presented here is for the dual-stage servo system with a rotational or translational MA and an instrumented suspension [24].

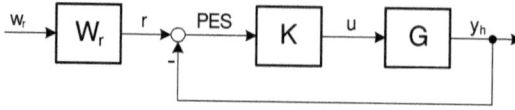

Figure 4.1: Block diagram of a SISO HDD servo

4.1.1 Performance Optimization

The major performance criterion of a disk drive system is the magnitude of the PES. We want to minimize the root mean square (RMS) value of the PES in the time domain so that data reading and writing can be performed correctly, or on the other hand, more data tracks can be put in a certain radial span resulting in a higher track density. For the SISO system shown in Fig. 4.1, we have the following relation of criteria between the time domain and the frequency domain

$$
\begin{aligned}
[\text{RMS}(\text{PES}(t))]^2 &= \lim_{T\to\infty} \frac{1}{2T} \int_{-T}^{T} \text{PES}^2(t)\mathrm{d}t \\
&= \frac{1}{2\pi} \int_{-\infty}^{\infty} |S(j\omega)|^2\, D_w(j\omega)\mathrm{d}\omega \\
&= \|W_r S(K)\|_2^2\,,
\end{aligned}
\tag{4.1}
$$

where

$$
D_w(j\omega) = W_r^*(j\omega) W_r(j\omega)\,,
\tag{4.2}
$$

and $S(K)$ is the sensitivity function of the controller K. In other words, the minimization of the RMS of the PES in the time domain is equivalent to the minimization of the H_2 norm of the sensitivity function multiplied by the disturbance weighting function

$$
\min_K \text{RMS}(\text{PES}(t)) \;\Leftrightarrow\; \min_K \|W_r S(K)\|_2\,.
\tag{4.3}
$$

In the MIMO case as shown in Fig. 2.7, we have the following relation:

$$
\min_K \text{RMS}(\text{PES}(t)) \;\Leftrightarrow\; \min_K \|G_{z_2 w_2}\|_2\,,
\tag{4.4}
$$

where each element of w_2 has already been normalized, and the bounds on control inputs have also been incorporated.

4.1.2 Stability Robustness

Stability robustness is an important issue for practical implementation of hard disk servo controllers. A designed controller should retain stability over a batch of drives, that is, should exhibit adequate stability robustness to plant variation. To this end, both qualitative and quantitative information about plant uncertainty should be known to some extent and be brought into consideration during the design process. In SISO design approaches, as presented in Sections 3.2 and 3.3, stability robustness is mainly described by

gain and phase margins. However, gain/phase margins are obviously inadequate to characterize stability robustness for MIMO systems, since inter-coupling dynamics between
system states and between subsystems can more easily consume the nominal gain/phase
margins and make the perturbed closed-loop system unacceptable or even unstable.

In robust control theories, stability robustness of a system is characterized by either
the H_∞ norm or the structured singular value (μ), which is essentially derived from the
small gain theorem. The H_∞ measure is suitable to deal with uncertainty blocks that are
almost full complex, or not so structured; while μ is more general and can handle highly
structured uncertainty blocks. Therefore, μ-synthesis can consider both real parametric
and complex dynamic uncertainties simultaneously, at the cost of an even higher controller
order so as to take into account the structural information of the uncertainty block. The
H_∞ norm of a system G is defined as

$$\|G\|_\infty := \max_{\omega \in \mathbf{R}} \bar{\sigma}\left[G(j\omega)\right].$$ (4.5)

Given an uncertainty block set $\mathbf{\Delta}$, such as the one defined in (2.10), for a plant G, $\mu_\mathbf{\Delta}(G)$
is defined to be [4]

$$\mu_\mathbf{\Delta}(G) := \frac{1}{\min\left\{\bar{\sigma}(\Delta) : \Delta \in \mathbf{\Delta}, \det(I - G\Delta) = 0\right\}}$$ (4.6)

unless no $\Delta \in \mathbf{\Delta}$ makes $I - G\Delta$ singular, in which case $\mu_\mathbf{\Delta}(G) := 0$.

To reduce the gap between the H_∞ norm and μ when characterizing a plant's stability robustness, we want to have a low-dimensional Δ block for mixed H_2/H_∞ synthesis.
Multiplicative dynamic (complex) uncertainties of the two actuators, the VCM and MA,
are therefore considered, yielding a 2-by-2 diagonal, complex Δ block as shown in Fig. 2.7

$$\Delta = \begin{bmatrix} \Delta_V & 0 \\ 0 & \Delta_M \end{bmatrix} \quad \text{and} \quad \sup_\omega \bar{\sigma}(\Delta(j\omega)) \leq 1.$$ (4.7)

From μ theory [4], it is well known that given condition (4.7), the closed-loop system
retains internal stability if and only if

$$\sup_\omega \mu_\mathbf{\Delta}\left(G_{\mathrm{cl}}(j\omega)\right) < 1,$$ (4.8)

where G_{cl} is the closed-loop plant as shown in the lower part of Fig. 2.7 except the
uncertainty Δ block at the top.

We also have the following bounds on $\mu_\mathbf{\Delta}(G)$

$$\rho(G) \leq \mu_\mathbf{\Delta}(G) \leq \bar{\sigma}(G),$$ (4.9)

where $\rho(G)$ denotes all eigenvalues of G. The upper bound can be achieved when G is
a full complex matrix. So, for the Δ block considered in this design, which is 2-by-2
diagonal, we can approximate condition (4.8) by two separate H_∞ norm bounds:

$$\sup_\omega \mu_{\mathbf{\Delta}_V}(G_{\mathrm{cl}}(K)) = \|G_{z_\Delta w_\Delta}(K, \Delta_V)\|_\infty < \gamma_V < 1,$$ (4.10)

$$\sup_\omega \mu_{\mathbf{\Delta}_M}(G_{\mathrm{cl}}(K)) = \|G_{z_\Delta w_\Delta}(K, \Delta_M)\|_\infty < \gamma_M < 1,$$ (4.11)

where γ_V and γ_M are the design parameters selected by the designer, and $G_{z_\Delta w_\Delta}(K, \Delta_V)$ means that the dynamic system $G_{z_\Delta w_\Delta}$ is explicitly dependent on the controller K and the multiplicative dynamic uncertainty Δ_V. The above two inequalities ensure that the closed-loop system is robustly stable with either uncertainty Δ_V or Δ_M applied separately. However, by making γ_V and γ_M less than one and small enough, eventually we can ensure that condition (4.8) is satisfied, which means that the closed-loop system is robustly stable when the uncertainties Δ_V and Δ_M take effect simultaneously.

4.1.3   Multi-Objective Optimization via LMIs

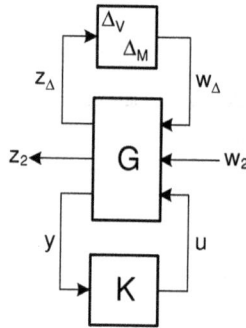

Figure 4.2: Block diagram of multiobjective optimization by mixed H_2/H_∞

By $\mathbf{K}(\mathbf{B}_\Delta)$, we denote the set of all controllers that stabilize the closed-loop system in Fig. 4.2 for $\Delta \in \mathbf{B}_\Delta$. Similarly, $\mathbf{K}(\mathbf{B}_{\Delta_V})$ and $\mathbf{K}(\mathbf{B}_{\Delta_M})$ denote the sets of all stabilizing controllers for $\Delta \in \mathbf{B}_{\Delta_V}$ and $\Delta \in \mathbf{B}_{\Delta_M}$, respectively, and $\mathbf{K}(0)$ denotes the set of all stabilizing controllers for the nominal plant. Then from the above discussion, we have shown that the controller design of a track-following servo may be cast as an H_2 norm optimization problem with some H_∞ norm constraints, that is, given a general plant G, we want to design an output dynamic feedback controller such that

$$K = \arg \min_{K \in \mathbf{K}(\mathbf{B}_{\Delta_V}) \cap \mathbf{K}(\mathbf{B}_{\Delta_M})} \gamma_2,$$

$$\text{subject to} \quad \begin{cases} \|G_{z_2 w_2}(K, 0)\|_2 < \gamma_2, \\ \|G_{z_\Delta w_\Delta}(K, \Delta_V)\|_\infty < \gamma_V, \\ \|G_{z_\Delta w_\Delta}(K, \Delta_M)\|_\infty < \gamma_M. \end{cases} \quad (4.12)$$

Now the problem can be cast into a standard mixed-norm optimization problem. With the aid of the LMI toolbox in MATLAB [10] and a highly efficient LMI solver called SeDuMi [56], this problem is readily solved and synthesized. The derivation of these LMIs will be presented in Appendix A.

4.1.4 Design Procedure

First, as in SISO design approaches, high-rate minor loop MA and VCM damping control is implemented, yielding G_{in} as shown in Fig. 3.1. Then this high-rate plant G_{in} is down-sampled to the low rate so as to accommodate the low sampling rate of the PES. In Fig. 4.2, G represents the generalized plant combining all frequency shaping functions. $\Delta = \mathrm{diag}[\Delta_V \, \Delta_M]$, $z_2 = [\mathrm{PES}\, u_v \, u_m]^T$, w_2 includes all disturbances, track runout w_r, and measurement noises $[n_1 \, n_2 \, n_3]$. $u = [u_v \, u_m]^T$, and $y = [\mathrm{PES}\, y_m]^T$. y_p is not used in y since it is found that this signal does not help much in the design of the outer loop low-rate controller K.

With the standard representation as in Fig. 4.2, we now can obtain the mixed H_2/H_∞ optimization problem as in (4.12). The set of inequalities can further be reformulated as a set of LMIs and then be solved by a convex optimization solver.

The main advantage of the mixed H_2/H_∞ synthesis method in disk drive servo design is that the computational cost is relatively low. It needs to solve only one convex problem with a relatively low dimension. While in robust H_2 synthesis, which will be presented later, iteration of solving convex optimization problems is necessary in order to approximate the corresponding nonconvex one. However, a disadvantage of mixed H_2/H_∞ synthesis is that it is unsuitable to deal with structured uncertainties because of the gap between the H_∞ norm and μ, as well as performance robustness. In other words, there is no guarantee that the claimed nominal performance is robust to plant uncertainties after the closed-loop system is obtained.

4.1.5 Design and Simulation Results

Dynamics of the Tracking Controller

The dynamic responses of the reduced-order controllers from the PES to the VCM control input u_v are shown in Fig. 4.3. Three controllers are considered for comparison: the first achieves H_2 norm minimization only, which is equivalent to the standard LQG design; the second achieves H_2 norm minimization with two H_∞ norm constraints, while the third is the reduced-order version of the second controller. Hankel model reduction is performed to obtain the reduced order controller [4].

From Fig. 4.3, it can be seen that the H_2 controller has multiple peaks and notches, especially in the high frequency range. These fine features are introduced by the mode shape of the actuator dynamics, disturbance weighting functions and uncertainty weighting functions. They are expected to shape the controller dynamics in such a way that the best tracking performance is achieved, i.e., the RMS value of the PES is minimized. However, system stability robustness is not guaranteed in this case. When the H_∞ norm bounds are imposed during the controller design process to guarantee robust stability, those high frequency peaks corresponding to actuator modes are greatly lowered, in order to attain more robustness when plant uncertainties become relatively large in the high frequency range.

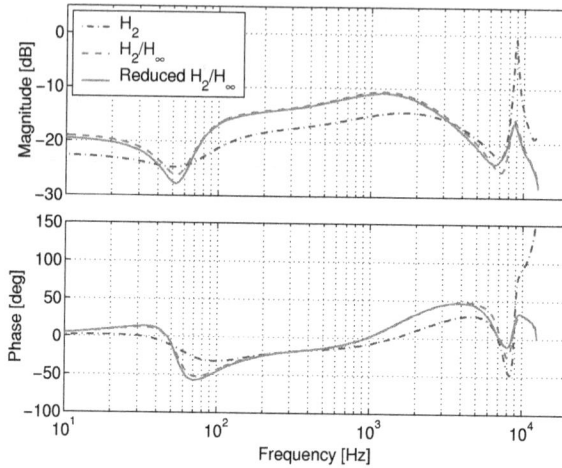

Figure 4.3: Bode plots of H_2/H_∞ controllers

Fig. 4.4 shows the Bode plots of the sensitivity transfer functions resulting from the three controllers mentioned above. The bandwidths for these systems are about 3 kHz. These curves are almost the same except in the low frequency range. Note that these sensitivity functions do not reflect the vibration attenuation effect in the inner loop, since structural vibrations are mainly excited by airflow turbulence rather than by track runout, and they are already dealt with by the inner loop vibration damping and compensation controller.

Robust Stability Analysis

The μ plots of the closed-loop system with respect to both individual and the combination of the uncertainties Δ_V and Δ_M are shown in Fig. 4.5. Since the magnitude of $\mu_\Delta(G_{cl})$ is always less than one, the closed-loop system is robustly stable under the presumed multiplicative uncertainties. The figure also shows that, when the two uncertainty channels take effect simultaneously, the resulting μ value (solid line) equals roughly the sum of μ values that result when each uncertainty channel takes effect individually, that is, $\mu_\Delta(G_{cl}) \approx \mu_{\Delta_V}(G_{cl}) + \mu_{\Delta_M}(G_{cl})$. This phenomenon explains why a tighter H_∞ norm bound should be assigned to each uncertainty channel, so that the final closed-loop system could still remain stable even when both uncertainty channels take effect simultaneously.

We can also check the stability robustness of the closed-loop system to parametric uncertainties using μ. In this analysis, parameter variations in the uncertain dual-stage actuator model are shown in Table 2.1. The subscript i denotes the seven off-track modes of the suspension. A larger variation ($\pm12\%$) is assumed for the MA's resonance frequency, which results from lithographic misalignment and variations present in etching processes.

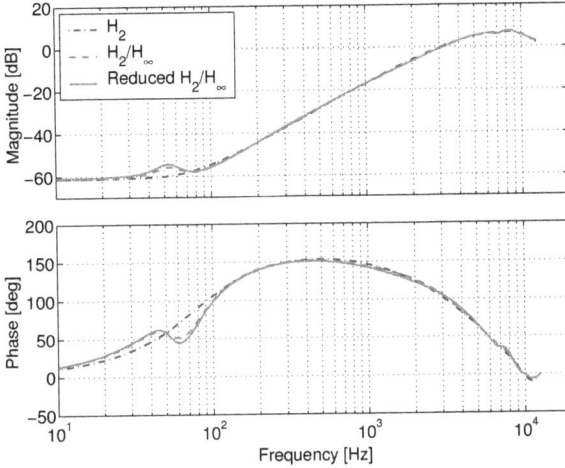

Figure 4.4: Bode plots of sensitivity transfer functions resulting from the three controllers

To begin the analysis, we first represent the full-order plant model as LFTs so as to incorporate parametric uncertainties. The two inner loop damping controllers are then closed around the plant to yield a damped plant G_{in}. This plant is then lifted from 50 kHz to 25 kHz before connecting to the low-order tracking controller. Lifting is an operation to obtain a lower sampling equivalent of a multirate system by grouping the fast sampled signals of the system, such that each group updates at the lower rate. By lifting, the inter-sample behavior, or the high-rate updating property of the damped system, is retained when connected to the low-rate outer controller. After the outer controller is closed around the damped plant, μ-analysis can be performed on the closed-loop system. Note that, by lifting, both the size of the diagonal Δ block and the repeatedness of each parameter are doubled. The lifting operation is illustrated in Fig. 4.6. The reader is referred to [4] for details on LFT modeling and μ-analysis.

Fig. 4.7 shows the μ plots for parametric uncertainties. In this figure, the first peak around 2 kHz corresponds to the MA mode variation. The two peaks around 6 kHz and 10 kHz results from the two dominant VCM/E-block/suspension modes: the butterfly mode and the suspension first sway mode, respectively. The last peak around 12 kHz reflects the suspension torsion mode around 13 kHz due to aliasing. By proper design and parameter selection, all these peaks are kept below 1, implying that the closed-loop system, with y_m and y_p used for damping, remains stable when all modes are included and with parameter variations shown in Table 2.1. We therefore conclude that the system is robust to high frequency spill-over and to some variations in modal frequencies and damping. It is also noted that, when y_m is not used for MA damping, the peak around 2 kHz is much higher with MA parameter variations. This implies that the system is unstable under some variation within the prescribed ranges. A re-calculation shows that when the

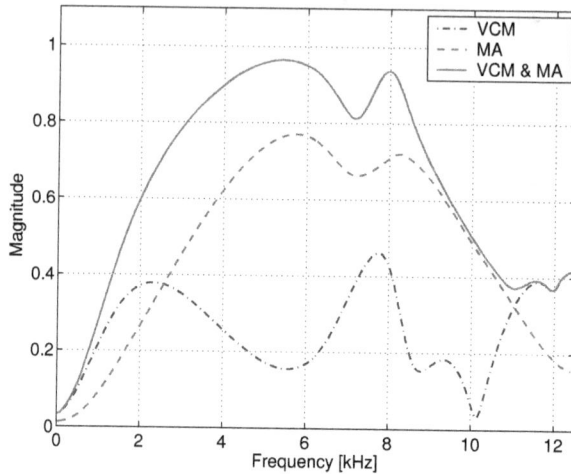

Figure 4.5: μ plots for different multiplicative uncertainties

MA damping is not used, the resulted closed-loop system can only withstand a maximum variation of $\pm 8\%$ of the MA resonance frequency. This deterioration results from the fact that there is mismatch between the characterizations of multiplicative and parametric uncertainty. Robust stability to the modeled multiplicative uncertainty cannot guarantee the same property for the modeled parametric uncertainty.

4.2 Mixed H_2/μ Synthesis

In the previous section, mixed H_2/H_∞ synthesis was presented, in which the Δ block was selected to consist of only two multiplicative complex uncertainties of the two actuators, so as to yield a low order for the general plant and the resulting controller. From (4.5), (4.6) and (4.9), we know that the difference between the H_∞ norm and μ of a system will become large if the dimension of the Δ block increases and the block is more structured compared to a full complex one. To solve this problem, it is desirable to characterize robust stability using μ instead of H_∞ norms during the design process. More freedom is then available to characterize plant uncertainties, including not only multiplicative dynamic uncertainties, but also real parametric uncertainties.

4.2.1 Incorporating Structured Uncertainty

In this section, mixed H_2/H_∞ synthesis is extended such that robust stability is characterized by μ rather than H_∞ norms. Parametric uncertainty can then be included in the uncertainty structure Δ for explicit consideration during the design process. The design procedure is similar to the D-K iteration in μ-synthesis with the alteration that the K

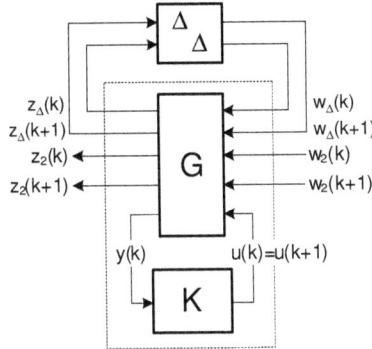

Figure 4.6: Plant lifting for μ-analysis of parametric uncertainties

part now is designed by mixed H_2/H_∞ optimization rather than by H_∞ optimization.

Let us first review some results from μ theory [4].

$$\mu_\Delta(G) \leq \inf_{D \in \mathbf{D}_\Delta} \bar{\sigma}(DGD^{-1}), \tag{4.13}$$

where $\mathbf{D}_\Delta$ is the set of matrices with the property that $D\Delta = \Delta D$ for every $D \in \mathbf{D}_\Delta$, $\Delta \in \mathbf{\Delta}$. For example, suppose that

$$\mathbf{\Delta} = \left\{ \begin{bmatrix} \delta_1 I_{2\times 2} & 0 & 0 \\ 0 & \delta_2 I_{4\times 4} & 0 \\ 0 & 0 & \delta_3 \end{bmatrix} : \delta_1 \in \mathbb{R},\ \delta_2 \in \mathbb{C},\ \delta_3 \in \mathbb{C}^{3\times 3} \right\}, \tag{4.14}$$

then $\mathbf{D}_\Delta$ is defined to be

$$\mathbf{D}_\Delta = \left\{ \begin{bmatrix} D_1 & 0 & 0 \\ 0 & D_2 & 0 \\ 0 & 0 & d_3 I_{3\times 3} \end{bmatrix} : \begin{array}{l} D_1 \in \mathbb{C}^{2\times 2},\ \det(D_1) \neq 0, \\ D_2 \in \mathbb{C}^{4\times 4},\ \det(D_2) \neq 0,\ d_3 \in \mathbb{C},\ d_3 \neq 0 \end{array} \right\}. \tag{4.15}$$

Using the upper bound in (4.13), the robust stability conditions in mixed H_2/H_∞ can be reformulated as

$$\min_{K \in \mathbf{K}(0)} \max_\omega \min_{D_\omega \in \mathbf{D}_\Delta} \bar{\sigma}\left[D_\omega F_L(G,K)(j\omega)D_\omega^{-1}\right] < 1 \tag{4.16}$$

$$\Rightarrow \min_{K \in \mathbf{K}(0)} \min_{D_\omega \in \mathbf{D}_\Delta} \max_\omega \bar{\sigma}\left[D_\omega F_L(G,K)(j\omega)D_\omega^{-1}\right] < 1 \tag{4.17}$$

$$\Rightarrow \min_{K \in \mathbf{K}(0)} \min_{D \in \mathbf{D}_\Delta} \left\|DF_L(G,K)D^{-1}\right\|_\infty < 1 \tag{4.18}$$

$$\Rightarrow \min_{K \in \mathbf{K}(0)} \min_{\hat{D}(s) \in \mathbf{D}_\Delta} \left\|\hat{D}F_L(G,K)\hat{D}^{-1}\right\|_\infty < 1. \tag{4.19}$$

By D_ω, we mean a frequency-dependent function D that satisfies $D_\omega \in \mathbf{D}_\Delta$ for each ω. Furthermore, we can restrict the frequency-dependent scaling matrix D_ω to be a real-rational, stable, minimum-phase transfer function, $\hat{D}(s)$, without affecting the minimum value of the H_∞ norm.

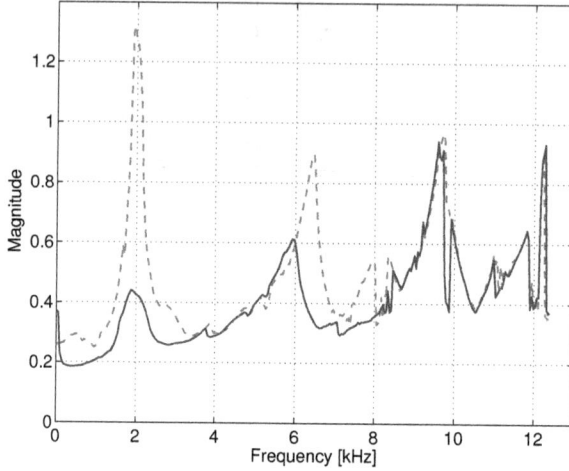

Figure 4.7: μ plots for parametric uncertainties

Now, by combining the H_2 performance term, we have the following problem setting for the mixed H_2/μ optimization problem:

$$K = \arg \min_{K \in \mathbf{K}(0), \hat{D} \in \mathbf{D}_\Delta} \gamma_2 \,, \tag{4.20}$$

$$\text{subject to} \quad \begin{cases} \|G_{z_2 w_2}(K, 0)\|_2 < \gamma_2 \,, \\ \left\| \hat{D} G_{z_\Delta w_\Delta}(K, \Delta) \hat{D}^{-1} \right\|_\infty < 1 \,. \end{cases} \tag{4.21}$$

By the Small Gain Theorem, we see that the constraint

$$\left\| \hat{D} G_{z_\Delta w_\Delta}(K, \Delta) \hat{D}^{-1} \right\|_\infty < 1 \tag{4.22}$$

guarantees the closed-loop stability for all $\Delta \in \mathbf{B}_\Delta$.

4.2.2 Design Procedure

Based on the above results, we take the following three-step procedure to solve the above optimization problem approximately.

1. Find a real-rational, stable, minimum-phase transfer function $\hat{D}(s) \in \mathbf{D}_\Delta$, as well as a controller K, that solves the optimization

$$\min_{K \in \mathbf{K}(0), \hat{D} \in \mathbf{D}_\Delta} \left\| \hat{D} G_{z_\Delta w_\Delta}(K, \Delta) \hat{D}^{-1} \right\|_\infty \,. \tag{4.23}$$

2. Using the $\hat{D}$ obtained in Step 1, solve the mixed H_2/H_∞ optimization problem

$$K = \arg \min_{K \in \mathbf{K}(0)} \gamma_2 \,, \qquad (4.24)$$

subject to $\left\{ \begin{array}{l} \|G_{z_2 w_2}(K,0)\|_2 < \gamma_2 \,, \\ \left\|\hat{D}G_{z_\Delta w_\Delta}(K,\Delta)\hat{D}^{-1}\right\|_\infty < 1 \,. \end{array} \right. \qquad (4.25)$

3. With the K found in Step 2, solve the following optimization problem

$$\min_{\hat{D} \in \mathbf{D}_\Delta} \left\|\hat{D}G_{z_\Delta w_\Delta}(K,\Delta)\hat{D}^{-1}\right\|_\infty \,. \qquad (4.26)$$

First, Step 1 is executed, yielding an initial scaling matrix $\hat{D}$. This is a standard μ-synthesis problem. With this scaling matrix obtained, we then solve a standard mixed H_2/H_∞ optimization problem as in Step 2, using the same technique as the one in Section 4.1.4. With the K found in Step 2, solve for the corresponding scaling matrix $\hat{D}$ as in Step 3, then go back to Step 2 and perform iterations between Step 2 and Step 3, until γ_2 does not decrease noticeably compared to some predefined tolerance. The iteration between Steps 2 and 3 is analogous to the D-K iteration in μ-synthesis, except that the K part in Step 2 is formulated as a mixed H_2/H_∞ optimization problem rather than an H_∞ one.

The main advantage of mixed H_2/μ optimization, compared to mixed H_2/H_∞ optimization, is the extra freedom provided by $\hat{D}$. Note that $\hat{D} = I$ reduces mixed H_2/μ to mixed H_2/H_∞. Because of this freedom, we would expect better nominal performance and stability robustness from mixed H_2/μ. However, one disadvantage is that the problem now becomes nonconvex, and therefore, the obtained solution may not be a global optimum, just as the D-K iteration in μ-synthesis. Another disadvantage is that the design process is computationally demanding, especially when the $\hat{D}$ is of high order for better curve fitting. A tradeoff between the order of $\hat{D}$ and $\hat{D}^{-1}$, and the designed controller order, is therefore necessary. It was our experience that even zero-order $\hat{D}$ and $\hat{D}^{-1}$ can satisfy the requirement of approximating μ by its upper bound fairly well. During the design process, we also found that the $\hat{D}$-K iteration has a poor numerical property. The closed-loop system tends to be singular after several iterations, even though balanced realization has been performed. So, usually the iteration process should be carried out no more than three times. Actually, even one iteration can yield a system that has satisfying performance. Finally, like the mixed H_2/H_∞ approach, there is no guarantee of performance robustness.

4.3   Incorporating Multirateness

In the previous mixed H_2/H_∞ design, minor loop high-rate VCM and MA damping was implemented first, then the outer loop servo controller was designed at a lower rate. Although the combination of minor loop high-rate compensators and the outer loop low-rate track-following controller yields a multirate controller, it is not multirate in the strict sense, that is, multirateness is achieved by sequential single-rate designs, not by an inherently integrated version. The property of high sampling rate of the two auxiliary signals, y_p and y_m, has not been fully exploited during the sequential design process. Since the generalized plant as shown in (2.24) is periodically time-varying, ideally, a set of controllers can be designed all at once, with each controller executed at a specific time instant within a time period. According to the availability of the output signals and control input updating, each controller in that set has the corresponding input and output dimensions.

4.3.1   Review of Multirate Control

There have been several schemes to incorporate multirateness in the design process. In [61], a high order controller is decomposed into two parts: the slow modes and the fast modes. The resulting multirate controller is composed of a fast-mode controller with a high sampling rate and several slow-mode controllers with a low sampling rate. During implementation, interlacing is performed by inserting these slow rate controllers into the high rate controller in order to have an evenly distributed computation load. By this kind of decomposition and interlacing, the amount of computation can be uniformly reduced. In [52], multirate control means high rate control input and low rate plant output. A zero-interpolator is introduced as an up-sampling scheme to convert the plant to a higher rate. Then conventional H_∞ is applied to optimize the system performance as well as to reduce the effect of aliasing noise caused by the up-sampling scheme. As for this type of multirate control, some other methods have been proposed, like the design based on multirate observer [16], and multirate control which aims to achieve a good approximation of the continuous-time controller [13]. None of them deals with multirate output or multirate input, and all of these plant models are SISO systems.

4.3.2   A Systematic Treatment of Multirateness

In this section, we will apply known controller design methods for time-varying systems to the system (2.24), thereby a multirate controller can be designed in the strict sense. The application of multirate control techniques to the design of controllers for dual-stage servo systems in HDDs was first explored by Ryozo Nagamune [41][42].

It is proven in [8][31] that many important control synthesis problems for time-varying systems can be solved in a very similar way to those for time-invariant systems. Moreover, for periodically time-varying systems, these problems can be reduced to finite-dimensional convex optimization problems, which can be solved by using efficient numerical solvers for LMIs.

Consider the following periodically time-varying system with a period T:

$$\begin{bmatrix} \tilde{x}(k+1) \\ z_\Delta(k) \\ z_2(k) \\ \tilde{y}(k) \end{bmatrix} = \begin{bmatrix} \tilde{A}(k) & \tilde{B}_\Delta(k) & \tilde{B}_2(k) & \tilde{B}_u(k) \\ \tilde{C}_\Delta(k) & \tilde{D}_{\Delta\Delta}(k) & \tilde{D}_{\Delta2}(k) & \tilde{D}_{\Delta u}(k) \\ \tilde{C}_2(k) & \tilde{D}_{2\Delta}(k) & \tilde{D}_{22}(k) & \tilde{D}_{2u}(k) \\ \tilde{C}_y(k) & \tilde{D}_{y\Delta}(k) & \tilde{D}_{y2}(k) & 0 \end{bmatrix} \begin{bmatrix} \tilde{x}(k) \\ w_\Delta(k) \\ w_2(k) \\ \tilde{u}(k) \end{bmatrix} \qquad (4.27)$$

By $\boldsymbol{M}$, we denote the diagonal stack of a set of periodically time-varying matrices $\tilde{M}(k), k = 0, 1, \ldots, T-1$, where $\boldsymbol{M}$ can be substituted by either one of the system matrices $\boldsymbol{A}, \boldsymbol{B}, \boldsymbol{C}$ and $\boldsymbol{D}$. For example,

$$\boldsymbol{A} := \begin{bmatrix} \tilde{A}(0) & & \\ & \ddots & \\ & & \tilde{A}(T-1) \end{bmatrix}. \qquad (4.28)$$

We also define a cyclic matrix which is of compatible size with $\boldsymbol{A}$ and defined by

$$Z := \begin{bmatrix} 0 & \cdots & 0 & I \\ I & & & 0 \\ & \ddots & & \vdots \\ & & I & 0 \end{bmatrix}. \qquad (4.29)$$

When Z is multiplied from its right by a periodically time-varying vector, it performs a one-step cyclic shift of the elements of that vector. We then construct the following auxiliary LTI system

$$\begin{bmatrix} z_\Delta \\ z_2 \\ y \end{bmatrix} = \begin{bmatrix} Z\boldsymbol{A} & Z\boldsymbol{B} & Z\boldsymbol{B}_2 & Z\boldsymbol{B}_u \\ \boldsymbol{C}_\Delta & \boldsymbol{D}_{\Delta\Delta} & \boldsymbol{D}_{\Delta2} & \boldsymbol{D}_{\Delta u} \\ \boldsymbol{C}_2 & \boldsymbol{D}_{2\Delta} & \boldsymbol{D}_{22} & \boldsymbol{D}_{2u} \\ \boldsymbol{C}_y & \boldsymbol{D}_{y\Delta} & \boldsymbol{D}_{y2} & 0 \end{bmatrix} \begin{bmatrix} w_\Delta \\ w_2 \\ u \end{bmatrix}, \qquad (4.30)$$

where all input/output variables should be viewed as the lifted, or grouped ones respectively. It is noted that the LTI system (4.30) is essentially different from the periodically time-varying system (4.27). To have an equivalent representation, the dimension of the shifting matrix Z should be infinite, and the stacked representation (4.28) should accordingly be infinitely long, even though the actual sequence $\tilde{A}(k)$, $k = 1, 2, \ldots$ is periodic.

By a combination of the theories in [8][31], we can deduce the following equivalence.

♣ A linear time-invariant controller

$$u = \left[\begin{array}{c|c} Z\boldsymbol{K}_A & Z\boldsymbol{K}_B \\ \hline \boldsymbol{K}_C & \boldsymbol{K}_D \end{array} \right] y \qquad (4.31)$$

stabilizes the time-invariant system (4.30), and satisfies an H_2 or H_∞ norm condition

$$\|G_{z_2 w_2}\|_2 < \gamma\sqrt{T},$$
$$\text{or} \quad \|G_{z_\Delta w_\Delta}\|_\infty < \gamma, \qquad (4.32)$$

where T is the system period. Here, the matrices in (4.31) are block-diagonal and they have the form

$$\boldsymbol{K}_M := \begin{bmatrix} K_M(0) & & \\ & \ddots & \\ & & K_M(T-1) \end{bmatrix}, \tag{4.33}$$

where "M" can be A, B, C or D, and the block sizes in Z are compatible with the block sizes in $\boldsymbol{K}_A$.

♣ A periodically time-varying controller

$$\begin{bmatrix} x_K(k+1) \\ \tilde{u}(k) \end{bmatrix} = \begin{bmatrix} K_A(k) & K_B(k) \\ K_C(k) & K_D(k) \end{bmatrix} \begin{bmatrix} x_K(k) \\ \tilde{y}(k) \end{bmatrix} \tag{4.34}$$

of period T stabilizes exponentially the time-varying system (4.27), and satisfies the norm condition

$$\begin{aligned} \|G_{\boldsymbol{z}_2\boldsymbol{w}_2}\|_2 &< \gamma, \\ \text{or} \quad \|G_{\boldsymbol{z}_\Delta\boldsymbol{w}_\Delta}\|_\infty &< \gamma, \end{aligned} \tag{4.35}$$

where $K_M(k)$ in (4.34) is obtained from (4.33). It is noted that the H_∞ norm for time-varying systems should be interpreted as ℓ_2-induced. By the above equivalence, we see that the H_2 or ℓ_2-induced norm optimization problem for a periodically time-varying system (4.27) can be converted into a standard H_2 or H_∞ control problem for an auxiliary LTI system (4.30), with the controller structure (4.31) and (4.33). The final periodically time-varying controller (4.34) can be obtained by decomposing the controller matrices as in (4.33).

4.4   Robust H_2 Synthesis

The previous two MIMO design approaches, mixed H_2/H_∞ and mixed H_2/μ optimization, only optimize the *nominal* performance with guaranteed robust stability. They do not consider performance robustness, and therefore, plant perturbation may degrade system performance to an unacceptable extent before the closed-loop system becomes unstable. In this section, a robust performance design approach, called robust H_2 synthesis, is introduced. This approach was based on the result in [29], and was first applied to the design of controllers for dual-stage systems in HDDs by Ryozo Nagamune [42]. The reader is referred to them for more details.

In the robust H_2 design approach, the worst-case performance, rather than the nominal performance, is optimized. The worst-case performance is defined with respect to real *parametric* uncertainties, but not dynamic ones. Due to this limitation, let us first define the set $\mathbf{B}_p$ for parametric uncertainties as

$$\mathbf{B}_p := \left\{ \Delta = \text{diag} \left[\delta_1 I_{r_1}, \ldots, \delta_p I_{r_{N_p}} \right] : \ \delta_j \in \mathbb{R}, \ |\delta_j| \leq 1, \ j = 1, \ldots, p \right\}, \tag{4.36}$$

in which each real parameter variation δ_j is repeated r_j times. Then the robust H_2 problem can be stated as follows. Design a controller K that stabilizes the closed-loop system for all $\Delta \in \mathbf{B}_p$, and minimizes the worst-case RMS value of z_2 against w_2 for all $\Delta \in \mathbf{B}_p$, i.e., solve

$$\min_{K \in \mathbf{K}(\mathbf{B}_p)} \max_{\Delta \in \mathbf{B}_p} \|G_{z_2 w_2}(K, \Delta)\|_2. \tag{4.37}$$

In order to apply the results in [29] to the general LTI plant (2.22), we need the following two assumptions, $D_{\Delta\Delta} = 0$ and $D_{y\Delta} = 0$. The first condition is trivial to satisfy for parametric uncertainties. The second condition is to ensure well-posedness of the control system, and is also satisfied in our problem. By absorbing the uncertainty block Δ, the uncertain system from $[w_2^T \ u^T]^T$ to $[z_2^T \ y^T]^T$ can be expressed as

$$\left[\begin{array}{c|cc} A^\Delta & B_2^\Delta & B_u^\Delta \\ \hline C_2^\Delta & D_{22}^\Delta & D_{2u}^\Delta \\ C_y & D_{y2} & 0 \end{array} \right], \tag{4.38}$$

where superscript "Δ" means that the corresponding matrix has incorporated the uncertainty Δ, and the system matrices are given by

$$\left[\begin{array}{ccc} A^\Delta & B_2^\Delta & B_u^\Delta \\ C_2^\Delta & D_{22}^\Delta & D_{2u}^\Delta \end{array} \right] = \left[\begin{array}{ccc} A & B_2 & B_u \\ C_2 & D_{22} & D_{2u} \end{array} \right] + \left[\begin{array}{c} B_\Delta \\ D_{2\Delta} \end{array} \right] \Delta \left[\begin{array}{ccc} C_\Delta & D_{\Delta 2} & D_{\Delta u} \end{array} \right]. \tag{4.39}$$

To incorporate the multirateness of the plant, we apply the treatment presented in Section 4.3.2. Then, for the auxiliary time-invariant plant

$$\left[\begin{array}{c} z_2 \\ y \end{array} \right] = \left[\begin{array}{c|cc} ZA^\Delta & ZB_2^\Delta & ZB_u^\Delta \\ \hline C_2^\Delta & D_{22}^\Delta & D_{2u}^\Delta \\ C_y & D_{y2} & 0 \end{array} \right] \left[\begin{array}{c} w_2 \\ u \end{array} \right], \tag{4.40}$$

we want to design an LTI controller of the form

$$u = \left[\begin{array}{c|c} ZK_A & ZK_B \\ \hline K_C & K_D \end{array} \right] y. \tag{4.41}$$

We remark that all the uncertain matrices in (4.40) are affine in Δ. Combining (4.40) and (4.41) yields the following time-invariant closed-loop system

$$
\begin{aligned}
G_{\mathrm{cl}}(\Theta, \Delta) &= \left[\begin{array}{c|c} A_{\mathrm{cl}}(\Theta, \Delta) & B_{\mathrm{cl}}(\Theta, \Delta) \\ \hline C_{\mathrm{cl}}(\Theta, \Delta) & D_{\mathrm{cl}}(\Theta, \Delta) \end{array} \right] \\
&= \left[\begin{array}{cc|c} ZA^\Delta + ZB_u^\Delta K_D C_y & B_u^\Delta K_C & ZB_2^\Delta + ZB_u^\Delta K_D D_{y2} \\ K_B C_y & ZK_A & ZK_B D_{y2} \\ \hline C_2^\Delta + D_{2u}^\Delta K_D C_y & D_{2u}^\Delta K_C & D_{22}^\Delta + D_{2u}^\Delta K_D D_{y2} \end{array} \right],
\end{aligned}
\tag{4.42}
$$

where

$$\Theta := \left[\begin{array}{cc} K_A & K_B \\ K_C & K_D \end{array} \right]. \tag{4.43}$$

Our task is to find a robustly stabilizing controller matrix Θ that solves

$$\min_{\Theta} \max_{\Delta \in \mathbf{B}_p} \|G_{\mathrm{cl}}(\Theta, \Delta)\|_2. \tag{4.44}$$

This problem can be solved through optimization involving a finite number of matrix inequalities

$$\min_{\boldsymbol{W},\boldsymbol{P},\Theta} \gamma,$$

$$\text{subject to} \begin{cases} \gamma > \text{trace}\{\boldsymbol{W}\}, \\ \begin{bmatrix} \boldsymbol{W} & C_{\text{cl}}(\Theta,\Delta_k) & D_{\text{cl}}(\Theta,\Delta_k) \\ * & \boldsymbol{P} & 0 \\ * & * & I \end{bmatrix} > 0, \\ \begin{bmatrix} \boldsymbol{P}_Z & \boldsymbol{P}_Z A_{\text{cl}}(\Theta,\Delta_k) & \boldsymbol{P}_Z B_{\text{cl}}(\Theta,\Delta_k) \\ * & \boldsymbol{P} & 0 \\ * & * & I \end{bmatrix} > 0, \end{cases} \tag{4.45}$$

where $\Delta_k \in \mathcal{V}(\mathbf{B}_p)$ for $k = 1, \ldots, 2^p$. Here, the matrices $\boldsymbol{P}$ and $\boldsymbol{W}$ are block-diagonal of appropriate sizes, $\boldsymbol{P}_Z := \boldsymbol{Z}^T \boldsymbol{P} \boldsymbol{Z}$, $\mathcal{V}(\mathbf{B}_p)$ is the set of all vertices of the convex polyhedron $\mathbf{B}_p$, and symbol "*" denotes the transpose of the corresponding element at its transposed position. The replacement of infinitely many inequality constraints for $\Delta \in \mathbf{B}_p$ by finitely many ones at the vertices $\Delta_k \in \mathbf{B}_p$ is made possible by the facts that the set $\mathbf{B}_p$ is a convex polyhedron, and that the closed-loop system matrices in (4.42) are affine in Δ, therefore the worst-case performance will be achieved at one of the vertices of $\mathbf{B}_p$. The first fact comes from the restriction that only real parametric uncertainties are considered in the design, and the second fact is from the condition $D_{\Delta\Delta} = 0$ and hence (4.39).

This problem is nonconvex, since $\boldsymbol{P}$ and Θ are coupled in (4.45). However, by performing $\boldsymbol{P}$-Θ iteration which is similar to the D-K iteration in μ-synthesis, we can find a local optimum. First, we need to find an initial dynamic controller Θ, then we perform the following iteration procedure:

- Holding Θ fixed, solve the convex optimization problem (4.45) with respect to γ, $\boldsymbol{W}$ and $\boldsymbol{P}$.

- Holding $\boldsymbol{P}$ fixed, solve the convex optimization problem (4.45) with respect to γ, $\boldsymbol{W}$ and Θ.

The reader is referred to [29][42] for more details on finding a feasible initial Θ. As for the standard D-K iteration, each step in this $\boldsymbol{P}$-Θ iteration can be shown to improve the robust performance cost γ, but there is no guarantee to expect convergence to the global optimum.

The advantage of robust H_2 is the ability to cope with robust performance directly in the design. However, only real parametric uncertainties can be considered and we have to ignore complex or dynamic ones. Dynamic uncertainty can characterize high frequency unmodeled dynamics, which are common and sometime indispensable when modeling a physical system. In addition, the corresponding memory and computation are demanding. This results from the following two facts. First, we have to solve a series of convex optimization problems iteratively so as to approximately solve a nonconvex optimization one.

Second, the number of inequality constraints increases exponentially with the number of parametric uncertainties, since the constraints are imposed at all vertices of the polyhedron $\mathbf{B}_p$, which are counted up to 2^p. Therefore, only a few parametric uncertainties can be considered in the design.

4.5 Controller Order Reduction

All of the three MIMO design approaches presented in this chapter are applied to the generalized dual-stage plant model in the state space. When multirateness is incorporated in the designs, the final outcome is a set of periodically time-varying controllers with the same order as the generalized plant model. For both memory and computation saving, it is often desirable to approximate the state-space representation of these high order controllers with some lower order state-space representation, without significantly degrading system performance and stability robustness. Controller order reduction can be applied to standard time-invariant discrete-time systems based on balanced realization and some model reduction techniques such as Hankel model reduction. For periodically time-varying discrete-time systems, the cyclic reformulation by the accordingly-defined Z matrix can be applied to reformulate the periodic model reduction problem as a standard mode reduction problem for time-invariant discrete-time systems. An approach called balanced truncation model reduction approach is applied to those MIMO periodically time-varying controllers to obtain reduced-order ones. The reader is referred to [58] for more details.

Chapter 5

Comparative Studies of Various Dual-Stage Servo Systems

The previous two chapters discussed the design of dual-stage servo systems using SISO design approaches and MIMO design ones respectively. For SISO designs, high rate inner loop damping control is first implemented using the auxiliary sensor signals. Subsequently, a low rate outer loop controller is designed for the damped plant. For MIMO designs, multirateness has been naturally incorporated into the design process, and a set of controllers, which is periodically time-varying due to multirateness, is designed by explicitly considering plant uncertainty and hence robust stability. All of these design methods can be applied to the dual-stage multi-sensing system with either a rotational or a translational MA. By making detailed analysis and comparison of these designed dual-stage servo systems from various aspects, we can gain a better understanding of the difference between rotational and translational MAs, and also the advantages and disadvantages of each of these design methods, as well as guidelines for their practical implementation.

5.1 Rotational MA versus Translational MA

There have been two types of MEMS MAs: rotational [20] and translational [21][44]. In working principle, the difference between them can be solely expressed by the coupling dynamics G_C, as illustrated in Fig. 2.2. When the MA is rotational, $G_C = 1$; while if the MA is translational, then G_C has the form as in (2.3) and its frequency response is shown in Fig. 2.4.

To investigate the difference in track-following performance between the two types of dual-stage actuators, a comparative study through simulation is carried out. Two design methods are used: the SD design method and the mixed H_2/H_∞ optimization method. For both plants, inner loop MA damping by using y_m and VCM/suspension damping by using y_p are first applied. Then outer loop track-following controllers are designed by using the two methods and are closed around the two damped plants.

Time-domain simulations are carried out for the four closed-loop systems. In simulation, the time sequence of the reference signal, r, is generated from a combination of various sources, such as repeatable track runout (RRO), disk flutter, low frequency torque disturbances to the VCM, etc. Independently generated windage sources act on all suspension resonance modes. Measurement noises are injected into the system at proper locations. The strain sensor signal has a signal-to-noise ratio (SNR) of 35 dB and the relative motion of the MA has a measurement noise level of 1 nm (RMS value). The PES also has a measurement noise level of 1 nm.

During simulation, adaptive feedforward compensation by using y_p is applied to the MA, in order to compensate for the airflow excited suspension vibrations showing up in the PES. The adaptation mechanism can account for parameter variations of the suspension and the MA. Three parameter settings are specified by Table 5.1, which are just the three extreme cases within the parameter uncertainty range as defined in Table 2.1.

Figs. 5.1∼5.4 show the simulation results for various configurations, in which FF means adaptive feedforward compensation of the MA using y_p. Comparing Figs. 5.1 and 5.2, we see significant differences between the rotational and translational MAs, especially in the high frequency range. There are almost no resonance modes showing up in Fig. 5.2 due to the filtering effect of G_C. Comparing Figs. 5.1 and 5.3, we see that mixed H_2/H_∞ design achieves better performance than SD design by optimally shaping the sensitivity function and by making a better balance between the attenuation of r and w_v. From Figs. 5.2 and 5.4, we can see more clearly the improvement by optimal frequency shaping.

Table 5.2 summarizes the time-domain simulation results. In that table, the total PES has been decomposed into two parts: PES(w_v) and PES(r), where PES(w_v) is the PES resulting from airflow turbulence excitation, and PES(r) donates the remaining PES resulting from all other disturbance sources. With this decomposition, we can more clearly see the improvement by adaptive feedforward compensation. In the table, "R" and "T" denote the rotational and translational MAs respectively. Two aforementioned design methods are employed: the SD design method and the H_2/H_∞ optimization method. Those values expressed in percentage indicate the improvements that are achieved by adaptive feedforward compensation compared to the cases without FF, which are shown in the left columns.

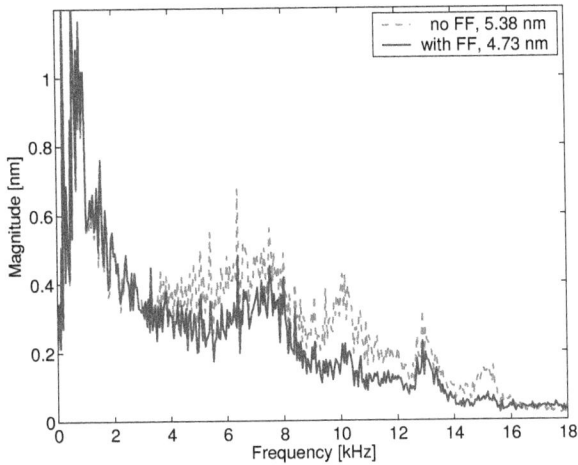

Figure 5.1: Power spectra of the PES (rotational MA and SD design)

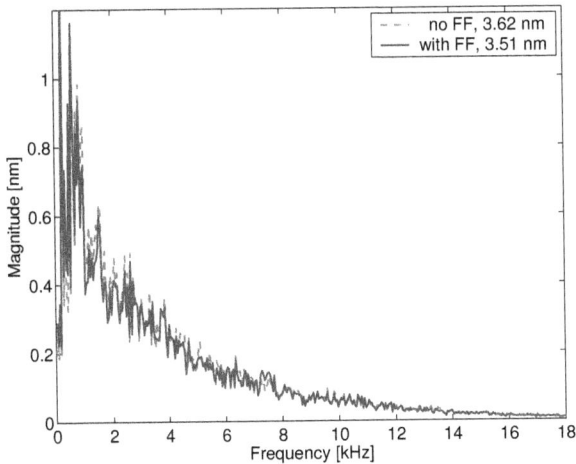

Figure 5.2: Power Spectra of the PES (translational MA and SD design)

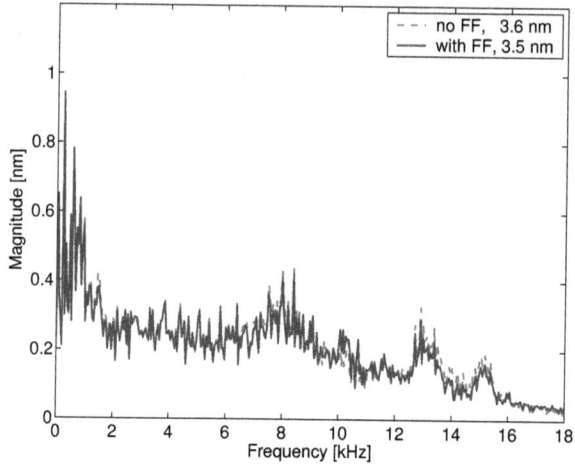

Figure 5.3: Power spectra of the PES (rotational MA and mixed H_2/H_∞ design)

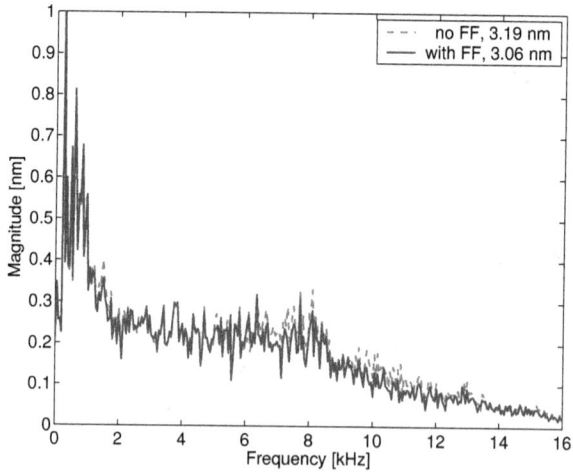

Figure 5.4: Power Spectra of the PES (translational MA and mixed H_2/H_∞ design)

Table 5.1: Parameter Variations of Plant Resonance Modes

Parameters	Three Cases		
	Minimum	Nominal	Maximum
VCM natural frequency (ω_i)	- 8%	0	+ 8%
MA natural frequency (ω_m)	-12%	0	+12%
Damping coefficient (ζ_i, ζ_m)	-20%	0	+20%
Modal constant (A_i, A_m)	- 5%	0	+ 5%

Table 5.2: Performance comparison between the two dual-stage actuators and the two control design methods (time-domain simulation)

Plant type	Parameter variation	Tracking controller	PES(r) [nm]		PES(w_v) [nm]		total PES [nm]	
			no FF	with FF	no FF	with FF	no FF	with FF
R	Nom	SD	3.62	3.57	3.98	3.10 (22%)	5.38	4.73 (12%)
T	Nom	SD	3.49	3.51	0.96	0.65 (32%)	3.62	3.57 (2%)
R	Min	H_2/H_∞	2.75	2.73	2.75	2.53 (8%)	3.89	3.72 (5%)
R	Nom	H_2/H_∞	2.77	2.74	2.32	2.18 (6%)	3.61	3.50 (3%)
R	Max	H_2/H_∞	2.99	2.93	2.46	2.09 (15%)	3.87	3.60 (7%)
T	Min	H_2/H_∞	2.81	2.82	1.90	1.40 (26%)	3.39	3.15 (7%)
T	Nom	H_2/H_∞	2.78	2.78	1.56	1.28 (18%)	3.19	3.06 (4%)
T	Max	H_2/H_∞	2.81	2.79	1.67	1.35 (19%)	3.27	3.10 (5%)

Several conclusions can be drawn from Tab. 5.2.

1. The translational MA case always performs better than the rotational MA case in the attenuation of airflow excited suspension vibrations, no matter what kind of design approach is used. We also see that this improvement is mainly achieved by reducing PES(w_v) with little change in PES(r). Obviously this is attributed to the mechanical, or passive, filtering effect of the translational MA on suspension vibration.

2. The mixed H_2/H_∞ design achieves better performance than the SD design by making a better tradeoff between the attenuation of PES(r) and PES(w_v). For the R-N case, both PES(r) and PES(w_v) are reduced by the H_2/H_∞ design, while for the T-N case, the H_2/H_∞ design reduces PES(r) significantly by amplifying PES(w_v) a little, producing a smaller total PES. This trend can also be seen from Figs. 5.1~5.4. A better tradeoff between PES(r) and PES(w_v) implies that the final PES becomes closer to a white noise and there is less room for further reduction.

3. Adaptive feedforward compensation can further attenuate PES(w_a), especially when there is plant variation. The effectiveness of feedforward compensation is affected by several factors: the order, or the tap number, of the compensator K_{MF}, the sampling rate of y_p, and the SNR of y_p. With more tap coefficients, the FIR is closer to an ideal IIR, which can be designed by LQG, and more modes can be taken care of by the compensator. With a higher sampling rate, the compensator will be able to deal with high frequency resonance modes effectively. During practical implementation, the strain sensor may pick up some resonance modes that do not contribute to the head offtrack motion. These modes are called non-offtrack modes. In feedforward compensation, they just appear as measurement noise to deteriorate the compensation performance. Optimization in sensor location and orientation is therefore necessary to improve the SNR for better vibration compensation [45].

4. The combination of the H_2/H_∞ design and adaptive feedforward compensation can achieve the best performance with fairly good performance robustness. For the rotational MA case, performance degradation under plant variation is less than 6%, while this degradation is less than 3% for the translational MA case. Again, the translational MA case achieves better performance robustness partially due to the coupling-filtering effect, which is very robust to parameter variation.

Some points should be noted on the time-domain simulation results. The disturbance model used in the simulation is based on the results from a single-stage system, which may differ from that of a dual-stage system when an MA is incorporated into the system. The MA resonance mode may be excited directly by airflow turbulence, which has already been modelled as w_m in design and simulation. But with the relative MA motion available for inner loop damping, this effect can be greatly reduced. Sensing noise is also an important issue. The claimed system performance relies on good sensing properties with a reasonably high SNR of y_m [60].

5.2 Comparisons of Robust H_2 Performance in the Frequency Domain

In disk drive servo systems, a necessary requirement is that the controller should robustly stabilize actual systems over plant uncertainties and variations. Stability robustness can be checked through μ-analysis. Fig. 5.5 compares the μ plots of the PQ design and the mixed H_2/H_∞ design for the dual-stage system with a translational MA. The high-rate damped plant is lifted before connecting to the low-rate controller, as illustrated in Fig. 4.6. Adaptive feedforward compensation is not considered in the analysis because it does not affect the system's stability. The maximum μ values are 0.8 for the PQ design and 0.93 for the H_2/H_∞ design, implying that both of the two systems are robustly stable with respect to the assumed parameter perturbation.

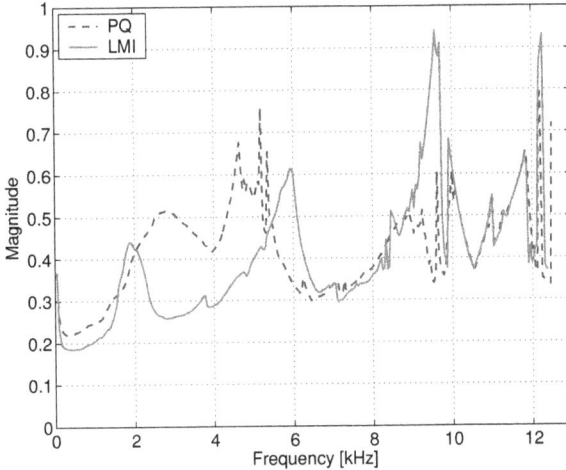

Figure 5.5: μ plots under parametric uncertainties of the two designs.

However, it is often not sufficient just to guarantee robust stability of a closed-loop system. Under certain plant variation, its performance may degrade to become unacceptable even though the system still remains stable. It is therefore important to have some knowledge of performance robustness of the system in the early design stage. Estimation of the worst-case performance can be conducted on the generalized plant with modeled uncertainty. One way of estimation is to use Monte Carlo enumeration, which will be used in the next section. In this section, we present an estimation method of the worst-case performance in the frequency domain [48][26]. This method uses a convex condition for robust H_2 performance in terms of an LMI across frequency. The main appeal of this method is that it provides the designer with frequency-domain insight into the worst-case performance of a closed-loop system.

Consider the system shown in Fig. 4.6. For parametric uncertainties, the Δ block has the same structure as defined in (4.36):

$$\mathbf{B}_p := \left\{ \Delta = \text{diag}\left[\delta_1 I_{r_1}, \dots, \delta_p I_{r_{N_p}} \right] : \ \delta_j \in \mathbb{R}, \ |\delta_j| \le 1, \ j = 1, \dots, p \right\}.$$

If Δ is LTI, then the uncertain closed-loop system $G_{z_2 w_2}(K, \Delta)$ is said to have robust H_2 performance level γ if it is robustly stable and

$$\sup_{\Delta \in \mathbf{B}_\Delta} \|G_{z_2 w_2}(K, \Delta)\|_2 < \gamma, \tag{5.1}$$

in which the H_2 norm is defined as

$$\|G\|_2 := \left(\int_0^{2\pi} \text{trace} \left(G^*(e^{j\omega}) G(e^{j\omega}) \right) \frac{d\omega}{2\pi} \right)^{1/2}. \tag{5.2}$$

This specification provides an adequate view of both uncertainty and disturbance. To estimate γ, define the sets

$$\begin{aligned} \mathbf{X} &:= \left\{ \text{diag}\left[X_1, \cdots, X_{N_p} \right] : X_i \in \mathbb{C}^{r_i \times r_i}, \ X_i > 0 \right\}, \\ \mathbf{T} &:= \left\{ \text{diag}\left[T_1, \cdots, T_{N_p} \right] : T_i = T_i^* \in \mathbb{C}^{r_i \times r_i} \right\}, \\ \mathbf{Y} &:= \left\{ Y = Y^* \in \mathbb{C}^{N_{w_2} \times N_{w_2}} \right\}. \end{aligned} \tag{5.3}$$

Suppose there exists $X(\omega) \in \mathbf{X}$ which is positive definite by definition, $T(\omega) \in \mathbf{T}$ and $Y(\omega) \in \mathbf{Y}$, such that

$$\begin{aligned} & j \left(\begin{bmatrix} T(\omega) & 0 \\ 0 & 0 \end{bmatrix} G\left(e^{j\omega} \right) - G^* \left(e^{j\omega} \right) \begin{bmatrix} T(\omega) & 0 \\ 0 & 0 \end{bmatrix} \right) \\ & + G^* \left(e^{j\omega} \right) \begin{bmatrix} X(\omega) & 0 \\ 0 & I \end{bmatrix} G\left(e^{j\omega} \right) - \begin{bmatrix} X(\omega) & 0 \\ 0 & Y(\omega) \end{bmatrix} < 0 \end{aligned} \tag{5.4}$$

holds for all $\omega \in [0 \ 2\pi]$, and

$$\int_0^{2\pi} \text{trace}(Y(\omega)) \frac{d\omega}{2\pi} < \gamma^2, \tag{5.5}$$

then the system $G_{z_2 w_2}(K, \Delta)$ is robustly stable and has a robust performance level γ.

The estimated results of $\text{trace}(Y(\omega))$ are shown in Figs. 5.6 and 5.7. The nominal H_2 performance ($\Delta = 0$) is also shown for comparison. The ratio between γ_{robust} and γ_{nom} is 1.59 for the PQ design and 1.35 for the LMI design, indicating better performance robustness for the H_2/H_∞ design. Also note that the major portions of the tracking error are located around 2 kHz and 5 kHz, which are consistent with the results shown in Fig. 5.5: performance degradation mainly results from the MA mode variation and decreased gain/phase margins.

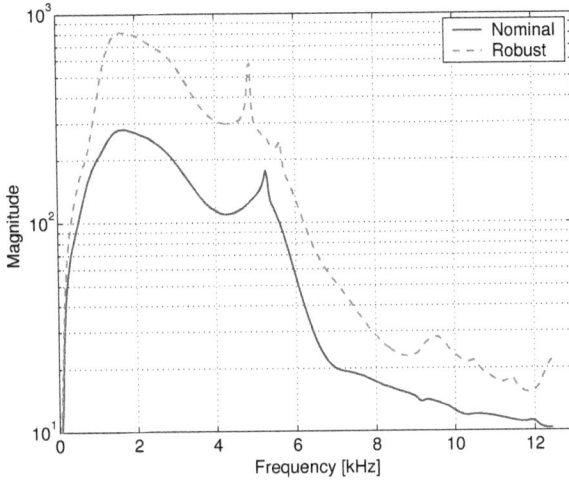

Figure 5.6: Robust performance estimation of the PQ design

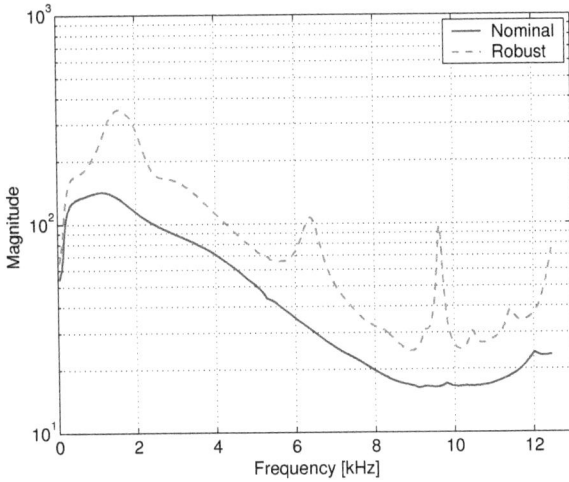

Figure 5.7: Robust performance estimation of the mixed H_2/H_∞ design

5.3   Comparisons between Multirate Control Systems

This section makes a detailed comparison between SISO and MIMO designs for the dual-stage plant with a translational MA [27]. We have seen that SISO designs use sequential loops with different rates in order to incorporate multirate sensing, while all MIMO designs can incorporate multirateness in a systematic way. Further, robust stability, or even robust performance can be explicitly considered in MIMO designs.

In all SISO and MIMO designs, the controllers were designed based on a simplified plant model, which includes two major VCM/E-block/suspension assembly modes and one MA resonance mode. However, the full-order plant model, which includes seven VCM-suspension assembly modes and the MA mode, was used in the simulation and evaluation of the designed controllers and closed-loop systems. Three criteria are checked on the full-order closed-loop systems: robust stability, nominal performance, and worst-case performance. In this simulation study, stability is checked by examining each system's complex poles, and nominal performance is obtained by solving a discrete Lyapunov equation for the closed-loop system in the state-space form. For this reason, adaptive feedforward compensation cannot be implemented. Instead, fixed feedforward compensator is designed. K_{in} is designed to have two outputs, one is fed to u_v for VCM damping, and the other to u_m for MA compensation.

The designed controller should robustly stabilize all perturbed plants with bounded parametric variations as defined in Table. 2.1. Here, 400 plant samples are formed by randomly choosing a set of parameters from their respective variation ranges. Unstable cases are then counted from the closed-loop systems by checking their eigenvalues. If all of these closed-loop systems are stable, then the worst-case performance can be obtained. Here, two performance terms are considered: the RMS value of the PES and the control input u_m. The magnitude of y_m is indirectly constrained by minimizing u_m, so that y_m does not exceed the allowable MA stroke. In the track-following mode, the VCM input u_v is usually very small compared to its capability designed for the track-seeking mode.

The simulation results are listed in Table 5.3. In that table, each robust H_2 result is labelled by a 3-element vector indicating the availability of the three measurements [PES y_p y_m]. A value of 1 means that the corresponding signal was used in the control structure, while a 0 indicates that the signal was not used. "Degradation" is computed for the worst-case performance with respect to the nominal performance. Model reduction has been performed before obtaining the final controllers. Several comparisons can be made between the various design approaches and the following conclusions can be drawn from them.

Table 5.3: Performance comparison between control designs

Unstable cases are counted based on 400 perturbed plants. 'Degradation' denotes the ratio of worst-case over nominal performance. The 3-element vectors for robust H_2 indicate the availability of the three outputs [PES y_p y_m].

Design Approach	Unstables (/400)	PES (nm)			u_m (mV)			Controller Order
		Nominal	W.C.	Degradation	Nominal	W.C.	Degradation	
PQ method	0	7.75	10.00	129 %	205	234	114 %	6
SD method	0	7.11	8.35	117 %	277	316	114 %	6
Mixed H_2/H_∞	0	6.57	7.82	119 %	201	216	108 %	8
Mixed H_2/μ	0	5.31	5.88	111 %	261	298	114 %	8
Robust H_2 [111]	0	5.93	6.47	109 %	275	310	113 %	9
Robust H_2 [101]	0	5.96	7.10	118 %	308	388	126 %	10
Robust H_2 [110]	0	6.09	7.97	131 %	239	309	129 %	10
Robust H_2 [100]	0	7.66	9.45	123 %	278	399	144 %	10

1. *Robust Stability:* All of the five design methodologies yielded closed-loop systems that are robustly stable under the assumed parametric uncertainty model defined in Table 2.1. For the two SISO techniques, robustness to mode variation is mainly achieved through the incorporation of the inner loop damping of the VCM and MA. For the three MIMO designs, stability robustness is incorporated in the MIMO controllers by imposing auxiliary H_∞ norm or μ bounds, or by considering parametric uncertainty directly.

2. *SISO designs:* As for the two SISO design approaches, the SD method achieves better performance than that of the PQ method, because the relative MA motion, y_m, is utilized in the design of the outer loop tracking controller for the SD design but not for the PQ design. However, the variance of u_m is much smaller in the PQ design than in the SD design. This is probably due to the fact that the PQ design methodology explicitly takes actuator interference into account.

3. *MIMO designs:* The mixed H_2/μ approach achieved the best nominal and worst-case performance of all three MIMO techniques. This is attributed to the precise characterization of robust stability criterion through μ, which makes the controller less conservative and its capability can hence be fully exploited. The robust H_2 design achieves moderate performance with the smallest performance degradation. This is mainly due to the explicit consideration of worst-case performance during the design process. Both of the two methods yielded controllers that perform better than the mixed H_2/H_∞ design, indicating the conservativeness introduced by the H_∞ norm bounds for achieving robust stability.

4. *SISO design vs. MIMO design:* It can be clearly seen that the MIMO designs always perform better than their sequential SISO counterparts, not only with respect to nominal performance, but also with respect to worst-case performance. Performance degradation due to parameter variations from nominal values also shows the same trend: it increases at a smaller rate for MIMO designs than for SISO designs. These results show that MIMO designs are more aggressive in optimizing system performance by better exploiting the coupling property of the MIMO system while still guaranteeing robust stability.

   It is also observed that the control input effort at the MA, u_m, is not necessarily larger in MIMO designs than in SISO designs. This implies that MIMO designs achieve small tracking error by optimizing their controllers rather than by putting more control effort into the system.

5. *Multi-sensing:* The effect of multi-sensing is also checked by comparing different sensing schemes. A comparison of the four cases of robust H_2 shows that the use of either y_m and y_p can improve system performance significantly, while using both signals can achieve the best nominal performance with the smallest performance degradation. The use of the relative position measurement y_m makes the MA more robust to its mode uncertainty, and also makes it possible to optimally distribute

the control effort between the VCM and MA. However, a dedicated vibration sensor can provide suspension vibration information at a higher SNR and hence is necessary during approaching the extremely stringent target, 500k TPI. Improvement by multi-sensing is also due to the fact that y_p and y_m are sampled at a higher rate than that of the PES. With only the PES available at the low rate, we see significant performance degradation compared to the three multi-sensing cases.

6. *Controller order:* Controller order reduction was conducted on all three MIMO controllers, so that they can be implemented on the DSP board. However, care must be taken during implementation. Since these controllers are MIMO and dynamically coupled, they may be more sensitive to quantization error than their sequential SISO counterparts. It should also be noted that these MIMO controllers are periodically time-varying, which means that a set of controllers are designed and the set of parameter values for each time-varying controller must be stored and retrieved. As a consequence, more memory is needed for storing the time varying parameters, in order to implement these controllers.

Fig. 5.8 shows the frequency responses of the nominal sensitivity transfer functions by the three MIMO design approaches: mixed H_2/H_∞, mixed H_2/μ and robust H_2. The sensitivity transfer function is defined from the reference input, or equivalently track runout, to the PES. These responses have almost the same peak gains with different closed-loop bandwidth. Higher bandwidth usually implies stronger attenuation in the low frequency range. So, the mixed H_2/μ design performs best and the robust H_2 design is better than the mixed H_2/H_∞ one. Fig. 5.9 shows the frequency responses of the nominal sensitivity functions of robust H_2 design with different sensing schemes. The first three systems have similar sensitivity responses, but with different worst-case performance as shown in Table 5.3. The last system with only the PES measurable has the worst error attenuation below its bandwidth, also there are drastic fluctuations beyond its bandwidth, implying bad performance robustness. All these observations are consistent with those conclusions drawn from Table 5.3.

5.4 TMR Sources Analysis with Projection to 500k TPI

In the disk drive industry, track following servos are traditionally designed in the frequency domain before a drive is built. Time domain performance characteristics are not evaluated until a prototype drive is built and servo code is implemented. With rapid increase in TPI, one by one generation of disk drives is being developed and batch fabricated. Prediction of future products performance is desired and often crucial. From prediction, one may roughly know what performance can be achieved with those technologies and improvements to be applied to the new product, and what are the main remaining problems or obstacles to further performance improvement. With the targeted 3σ PES of 5 nm,

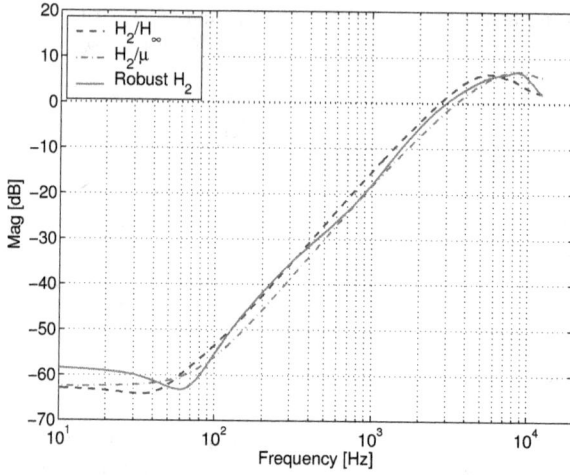

Figure 5.8: Frequency responses of the sensitivity transfer functions from the three MIMO designs

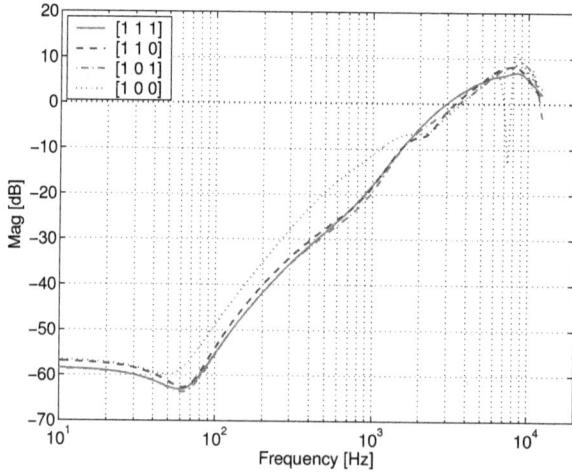

Figure 5.9: Comparison of different sensing schemes with the robust H_2 design approach

there is still a long way to go before achieving it. Much work has already been done on TMR sources identification, characterization and performance projection. Based on those results available at present, and the design methodology and simulation results for the dual-stage servo system presented in this paper, a more realistic performance projection can be performed.

First, TMR sources are decomposed and characterized in detail before doing performance projection. In general, TMR sources are classified into two categories: repeatable runout (RRO) and non-repeatable runout (NRRO). RRO is synchronous with spindle revolution and is caused by both imbalance in the spindle and imperfections in servo-written track circles, while NRRO is caused by various disturbance sources such as airflow turbulence, disturbances due to ball bearing defects, spindle and disk resonance modes, disturbance from adjacent disks, and external shock and vibration. In this study, TMR sources are classified into 6 items: 1) RRO; 2) disk runout, including disturbances from spindle and disk motion; 3) VCM torque disturbances, including low frequency (<2 kHz) disturbances from printed flex cable, spindle friction, spindle and disk resonance modes, and current amplifier nonlinearity; 4) Airflow excited suspension vibrations, which lie in the high frequency range (>2 kHz); 5) MA torque disturbance, which mainly result from airflow turbulence; 6) PES measurement noise, which is related to the PES demodulation noise and quantization noise. It should be noted that, the disturbance from adjacent disks and external shock and vibration are not included in the analysis. This is mainly because the two disturbance sources are difficult to characterize and project. They depend on the configuration of a specific hard disk drive and actual working conditions. As far as the authors are aware, till now there is no research result on the two disturbance sources that are published in the literature.

Performance projection is carried out based on the following assumptions.

1. Compared with ball bearing, a fluid bearing spindle will reduce spindle NRRO by a factor of 4 [14].

2. Disk flutter, arm torque disturbances and suspension vibrations decrease with $D^{1.4}$ [55][14][12], and airflow disturbances decrease with D^2, where D is the disk diameter.

3. Disk flutter is reduced by a factor of 3 due to the use of new disk substrate materials and the increase in its thickness [55][14].

4. By using a redesigned, stiffer suspension with higher vibration modes, the level of airflow disturbances is reduced by a factor of 2.

5. The PES measurement noise scales with the track pitch (fixed percentage of the track pitch) [9]

Table 5.4: TMR source decomposition with projection to 500k TPI.

Closed-loop TMR components (1σ value) Unit: [nm]	100k TPI 7200 RPM 3.5" disk	scaling	500k TPI 7200 RPM 3.5" disk	scaling	500k TPI 7200 RPM 2.5" disk	Open-loop TMR components
	Sampling rate = 25/50 kHz, Servo bandwidth = 2.1 kHz					
RRO (written-in runout)	3.578	1/4	0.895	1	0.895	141.12
Disk runout	1.867	1/4	0.467	0.62	0.290	13.96
VCM torque disturbance	0.385	1	0.385	0.62	0.239	128.84
Suspension vibration	3.711	1	3.711	0.62	2.301	4.10
MA torque disturbance	0.820	1	0.820	1	0.820	1.00
Measurement noise	1.209	1/5	0.242	1	0.242	1.00
Total RMS value	5.60		3.96		2.64	195.43
	Sampling rate = 40/80 kHz, Servo bandwidth = 3 kHz					
RRO (written-in runout)	2.050	1/4	0.513	1	0.513	
Disk runout	0.649	1/4	0.162	0.62	0.100	
VCM torque disturbance	0.151	1	0.151	0.62	0.094	
Suspension vibration	3.002	1	3.002	0.62	1.861	
MA torque disturbance	0.465	1	0.465	1	0.465	
Measurement noise	1.029	1/5	0.206	1	0.206	
Total RMS value	3.97		3.10		2.00	

The performance projection results are summarized in Table 5.4. These values are calculated from the time-domain disturbance sequences used in the simulation. The first scaling results from the combination of disk platter redesign, the use of fluid bearing, and the increase in TPI. Measurement noise reduction solely results from the increase in TPI. The second scaling is due to the reduction in disk size, which will reduce the airflow speed and turbulence level.

Another effective way of improving servo performance is to increase the sampling rate of the PES. This rate cannot be increased arbitrarily in practice, because it is determined by the hardware configuration: how much disk space is allocated for embedded track position information, or equivalently, for servo sectors. If this sampling rate could be increased, then the closed-loop servo bandwidth can be increased accordingly and high frequency disturbances will be less amplified. From the table we see that, when the dual sampling rates are increased from 25/50 kHz to 40/80 kHz, the tracking performance is improved by about 30%. Under a typical disk drive configuration, the servo sectors occupy about 5% of the total disk space. This means that doubling the number of servo sectors implies 5% more space required for servo sectors. During the continuous increase in track density, it seems feasible to allocate a little more disk space for position information storage.

The final point to be addressed here is that with all these scalings and improvements, airflow excited suspension structural vibration has become the most important contributor to the closed-loop TMR. This is partially due to the fact that structural vibrations are largely in the high frequency range and are difficult to be suppressed by the PES servo loop. Another reason is that little information on vibration suppression by mechanical design can be collected from the literature, because this is generally kept as a technique secret by disk drive manufacturers. But from the above projection results, we can still say that with substantial reduction in airflow excited structural vibration, it is possible to achieve the targeted track density of 500k TPI, or 3σ TMR of 5 nm.

Chapter 6

Modeling and Control Design of a Prototype Dual-Stage Actuator

This chapter presents the property characterization of two translational MEMS MAs and the control design for a prototype dual-stage actuator system with one of the two MAs. The experimental setup is first described. Dynamic properties of the system are tested and analyzed, validating the simulation model presented in chapter 2. Based on the identified model, a preliminary controller is designed using the PQ design method. Experimental results are finally presented.

6.1 Experimental Setup

Fig. 6.1 shows a picture of the experimental setup of the dual-stage servo system. It consists of a 7200-RPM, 3.5-inch form factor disk drive with a dual-stage actuator, a laser Doppler vibrometer (LDV), a digital signal processor (DSP) board, and a signal conditioning board. The disk drive has only one platter, and the MA is put beneath the disk with the attached slider facing up. This configuration avoids damaging the MA during the assembly process. An opening is cut in the sidewall of the disk drive to allow a laser beam from the LDV to shine onto the sidewall of the slider, so that the slider's absolute off-track motion can be measured by the LDV.

A floating-point DSP board from Digital Spectrum Inc., TMS320C6713 DSK, was used for signal processing and control implementation. An analog-to-digital convertor (ADC) daughter board from Texas Instruments (TI), THS1206 EVM, was connected to the DSK board though its daughter board expansion interface. We also designed a signal conditioning board, which fulfills the following functions: conditioning of the LDV signal output, digital-to-analog conversion (DAC), and VCM driving current generation. Fig. 6.2 depicts the structure of the experimental servo system.

Two translational MA samples, called MA-1 and MA-2 respectively, were designed and fabricated by Kenn Oldham. Some critical design parameters are as follows. The MAs are of size 3×3 mm^2. The nominal gap between two adjacent fingers is 4 μm with an allowable working stroke of 1 μm. The gain of electrostatic driving force is 77 μN/V.

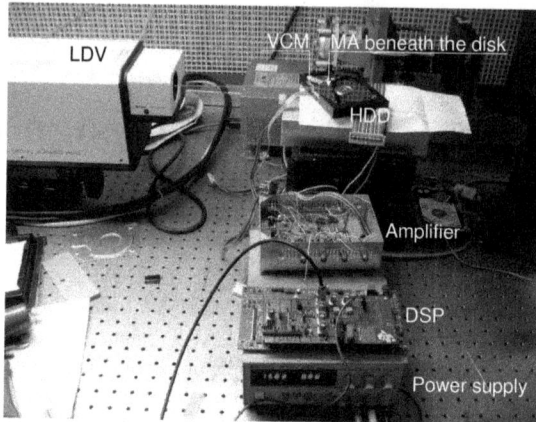

Figure 6.1: Experimental setup

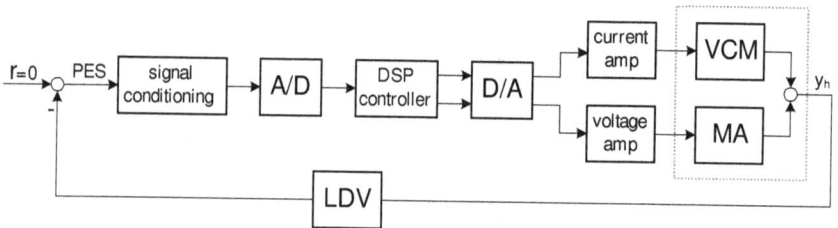

Figure 6.2: Block diagram of the experimental servo system

Two dual-stage actuators were assembled using the two MAs. However, the disk drive installed with MA-1 is not working properly due to a malfunction in its VCM. Therefore, both of the two MAs are going to be tested and analyzed, but only the disk drive with MA-2, called disk-2, will be used for servo control design and performance evaluation.

6.2   System Identification of the Dual-Stage Actuators

A dynamic signal analyzer, HP 35665A, is used to get the frequency response of a input-output channel by using sweeping sinusoidal as excitation input. The response data is collected by the LDV and then averaged to obtain a smooth response. The frequency response is obtained by taking the ratio between the input and its corresponding output.

In a dual-stage actuator with a translational MEMS MA, there is relative motion of the slider/head, y_h, with respect to that of the suspension tip, y_v, as illustrated in Figs. 2.1 and 2.2. In order to characterize the dynamics of the system thoroughly, y_h and y_v need to be distinguished and measured separately. Fig. 6.3 shows how the two signals are measured by adjusting the height of the laser beam slightly. When the laser beam is lowered just below the disk's bottom surface, which is the sidewall position of the slider, y_h is measured. When the laser beam is lowered a little further to the height of the MA sidewall, y_v can be measured. We can clearly see the difference between the two signals both in the time domain and in the frequency domain. For clarity, the transfer function from u_v to y_v is denoted as G_V, while the transfer function from u_v to y_h is denoted as G_H. As already defined, the MA response from u_m to y_h is represented by G_M.

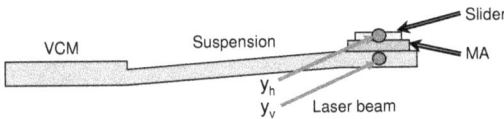

Figure 6.3: Measuring y_h and y_v by the LDV

6.2.1   Identification of the Two MAs

Figs. 6.4 and 6.5 show the measured and identified frequency responses of the two MAs, respectively. Due to some unknown reason, there are two, rather than one, peaks around the MA-2 resonance mode. The identified modal parameters are shown in Table 6.1, in which MA-2 is identified using both one-mode and two-mode models. It is seen that MA-1 has a lower resonance frequency with a larger damping ratio. This is probably because one supporting beam (spring) was broken during installation. The two-mode phenomenon of MA-2 is undesirable and should be avoided in the next batch of fabrication.

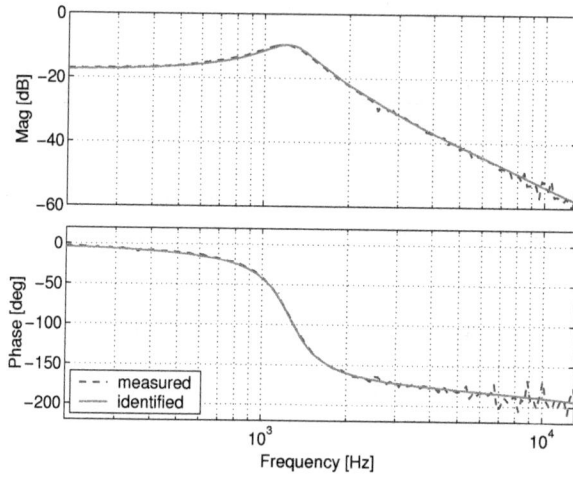

Figure 6.4: Measured and identified frequency responses of G_M-1

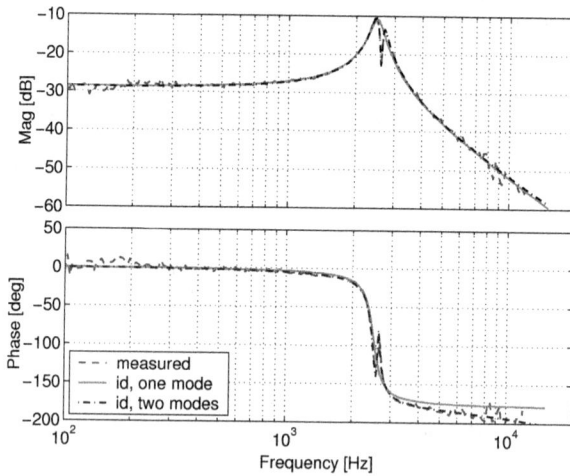

Figure 6.5: Measured and identified frequency responses of G_M-2

Table 6.1: Identified parameters for the MAs

	Natural frequency ω_m [Hz]	Damping ratio ζ_m
MA-1	1260	0.20
MA-2 (one mode)	2540	0.063
MA-2 (two modes)	2530	0.036
	2660	0.033

Table 6.2: Vibration comparison in various frequency ranges

Frequency range [Hz]		100~1k	1k~2k	2k~12.9k	Total
Disk-1	y_v [nm]	429.10	5.94	7.60	429.21
	y_h [nm]	450.59	11.66	2.71	450.75
Frequency range [Hz]		100~1k	1k~3.2k	3.2k~12.9k	Total
Disk-2	y_v [nm]	617.02	2.75	11.75	617.14
	y_h [nm]	641.91	9.27	6.13	642.00

6.2.2 Estimation of Airflow Excited MA Vibrations

When disk-2 is rotating at the nominal speed and its slider is flying, free off-track vibrations of the head and suspension tip, y_h and y_v, are measured. The plots of their power spectrum density (PSD) are shown in Figs. 6.6 and 6.7 respectively. From both figures, we can clearly see the filtering effect of G_C, as predicted in Fig. 2.3. Airflow excited high frequency suspension vibrations in y_v get significantly attenuated by G_C and there is little left in y_h. However, the magnitude of y_h around the MA resonance modes is bigger than that of y_v due to the resonance peaks of G_C.

Comparisons between y_h and y_v can be made in various (low, middle and high) frequency ranges. Table 6.2 makes such comparisons for the two disk drives. It is seen that in each high frequency range, vibrations in y_h are much smaller than in y_v, while vibrations are amplified from y_v to y_h in each middle frequency range. MA-1 has a stronger filtering effect than MA-2, since the former has a lower resonance frequency.

By using the single-mode model for each MA, the coupling dynamics of G_C, as defined in (2.3), can be derived, and their frequency responses are shown in Fig. 6.8.

For free vibration of y_h and y_v, we roughly have the relation

$$y_h = G_C y_v + w_m \,, \tag{6.1}$$

$$\Rightarrow \quad \hat{w}_m = y_h - \hat{G}_C y_v \,, \tag{6.2}$$

where w_m represents the MA vibration that is excited *directly* by airflow turbulence. With the estimated G_C models and the measured PSD of y_v and y_h, we can estimate the PSD of w_m using the relation (6.1) for both MAs. Figs. 6.9 and 6.10 show the estimated PSD of w_m for MA-1 and MA-2, respectively.

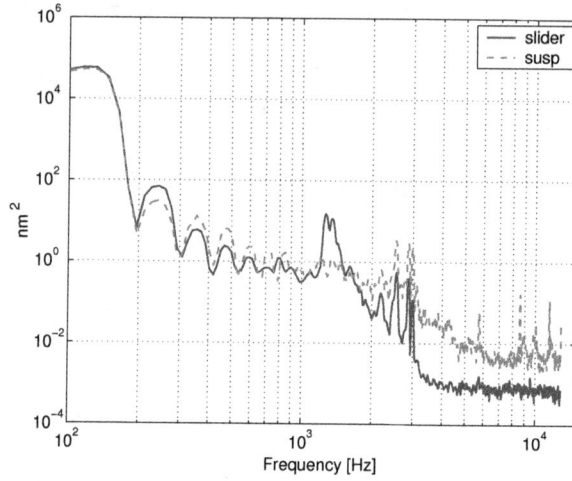

Figure 6.6: PSD of y_h and y_v in disk-1

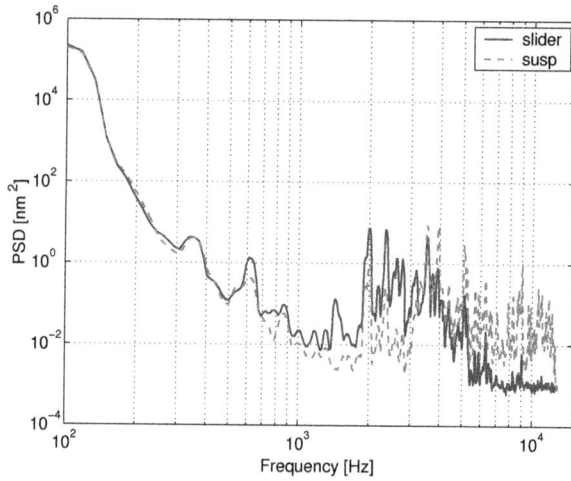

Figure 6.7: PSD of y_h and y_v in disk-2

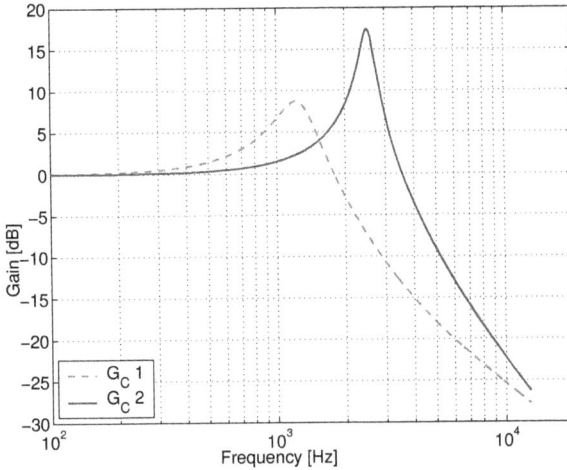

Figure 6.8: Simulated frequency responses of the coupling dynamics G_C

Due to measurement noise and error, and also possibly due to the correlation between w_m and y_v, the estimated PSD of w_m is not always positive. Obviously, those negative components do not make sense in terms of the PSD of w_m, which should always be non-negative. Therefore, to roughly estimate w_m, we only integrate the positive components around the MAs' resonance frequencies, as indicated in Figs. 6.9 and 6.10.

The estimated RMS value of w_m is 7.2 nm for MA-1, and 3.6 nm for MA-2. Relating the results with the ones in Figs. 6.6 and 6.7, we can conclude that with a lower resonance frequency of an MA, more head vibration is directly excited by airflow turbulence, and less vibration is transmitted from airflow excited suspension vibration. This phenomenon is reasonable, because with softer supporting beams or springs, it is easier to excite the MA's resonance mode.

6.2.3   Identification of the VCM/Suspension Assembly Model

Fig. 6.11 shows the frequency responses of G_V and G_H for disk-2. The two responses are related by the coupling effect G_C

$$y_h = G_H u_v = G_C G_V u_v = G_C y_v. \tag{6.3}$$

Using the $\hat{G}_C$ derived from $\hat{G}_M$, we can obtain an estimate of G_H from the measured G_V:

$$\hat{G}_H = \hat{G}_C G_V. \tag{6.4}$$

The measured and estimated frequency responses of G_H are shown in Fig. 6.12. Good agreement is observed between the two responses, implying accurate modeling and identification of the MA dynamics.

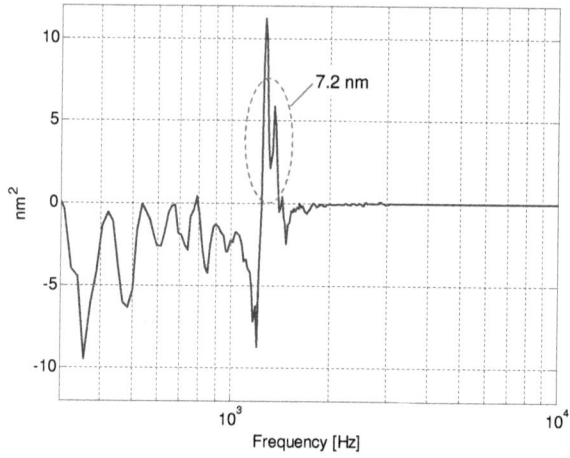

Figure 6.9: Estimated MA-1 vibrations excited directly by airflow

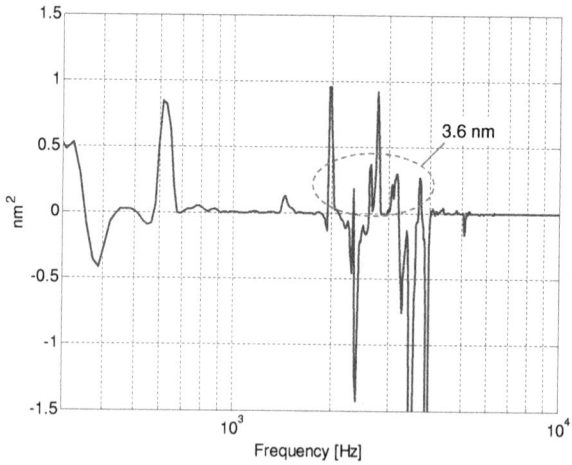

Figure 6.10: Estimated MA-2 vibrations excited directly by airflow

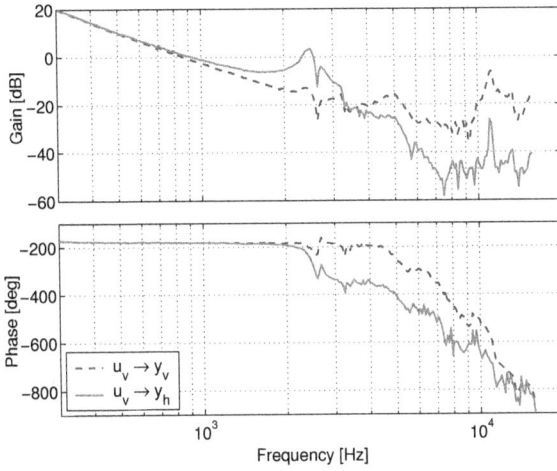

Figure 6.11: Measured frequency responses of G_V and G_H

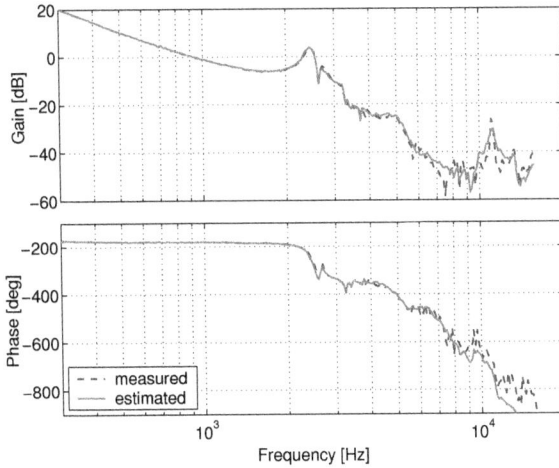

Figure 6.12: Measured and estimated frequency responses of G_H

Table 6.3: Identified parameters for the VCM/suspension/MA assembly dynamics

Mode	Frequency [Hz]	Damping coeff.
1	115	0.156
2	2540	0.034
3	2769	0.020
4	4879	0.053
5	5739	0.026
6	6432	0.018
7	8269	0.021
8	11233	0.006
9	14586	0.025
10	18051	0.021

System identification by curve fitting is also performed on the VCM/suspension/MA assembly dynamics. The identified modal parameters are shown in Table 6.3. The first mode is generated by the flex cable, bearing and friction. The second and third modes are the two resonance modes of MA-2. All remaining high frequency modes are suspension modes. Most of the suspension modes have a damping coefficient of about 0.02. The identified model will be used in the control design in the next section. Fig. 6.13 shows the measured and identified frequency responses of G_H.

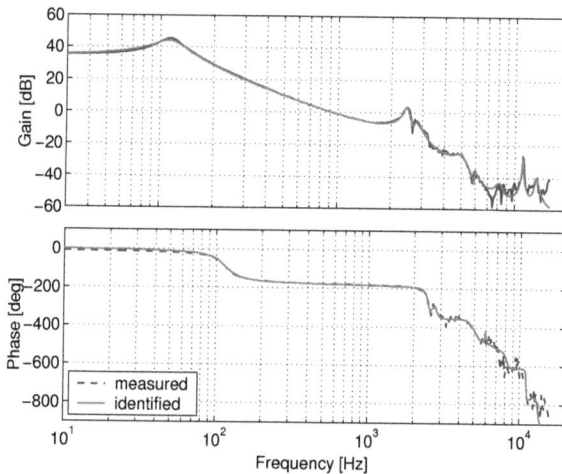

Figure 6.13: Measured and identified frequency responses of G_H

6.3 Preliminary Control Design for the Dual-Stage Actuator

6.3.1 Controller Design

The dual-stage actuator has only one output, y_h, which is measured by the LDV. Therefore it is a typical DISO system. We cannot design a controller for it using methods like the SD method, which needs to use the relative motion output y_m to decouple the two actuators. Here, a preliminary control design is conducted using the PQ method, which is applicable to DISO plants like the one we are dealing with.

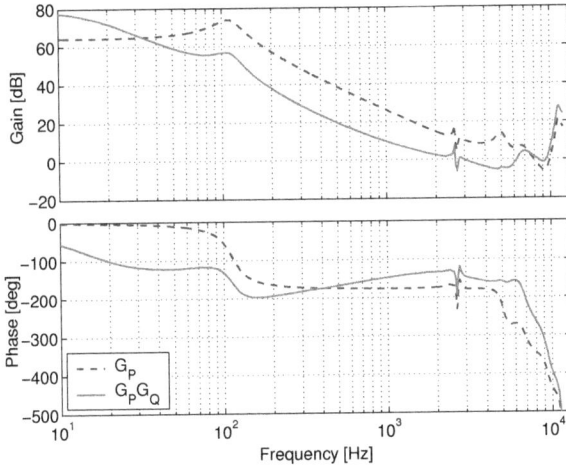

Figure 6.14: Bode plots of G_P and $G_P G_Q$

From the dual-stage model, we can derive G_P as defined in (3.13). Its frequency response is plotted in Fig. 6.14. A virtual controller G_Q is then designed to shape G_P. The low frequency gain is increased for more error rejection, and more phase margin is achieved to achieve better cooperation between the two actuators. The resulting frequency response of $G_P G_Q$ is also shown in Fig. 6.14.

6.3.2 Experimental Results

Fig. 6.15 shows the simulated and measured frequency responses of the closed-loop sensitivity function. There is good agreement in the high frequency range. The mismatch around 120 Hz is due to the variation of the bearing/friction mode of the VCM. Further increase of the closed-loop servo bandwidth is prevented mainly by the two closely related modes of the MA. Drastic phase change in this region results in high peaks of the sensitivity response, and makes the closed-loop system very sensitive to variation of that mode.

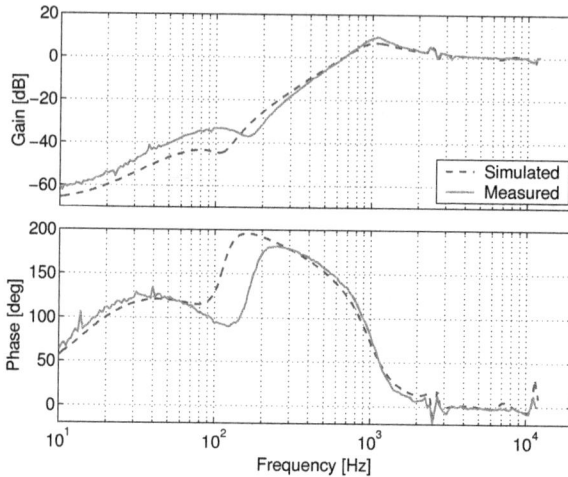

Figure 6.15: Measured and simulated frequency responses of the closed-loop sensitivity transfer function

However, the two-mode phenomenon is abnormal and specific in this MA. If we use a normal MA, an aggressive design can be made and better performance will be expected.

Fig. 6.16 shows the FFT of the PESs before and after control. This result matches well with the sensitivity response as shown in Fig. 6.15. Fig. 6.17 compares the two responses in the time domain, and Fig. 6.18 shows the time traces of the two control inputs, u_v and u_m. Comparing Fig. 6.17 with Fig. 6.18, we can see that the low frequency fluctuations in the open-loop PES are mainly compensated for by the MA, since a good match is observed between the time traces of the open-loop PES and u_m.

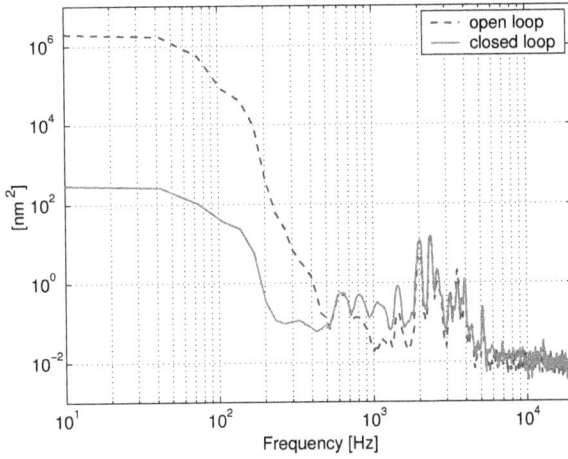

Figure 6.16: FFT of the measured PES

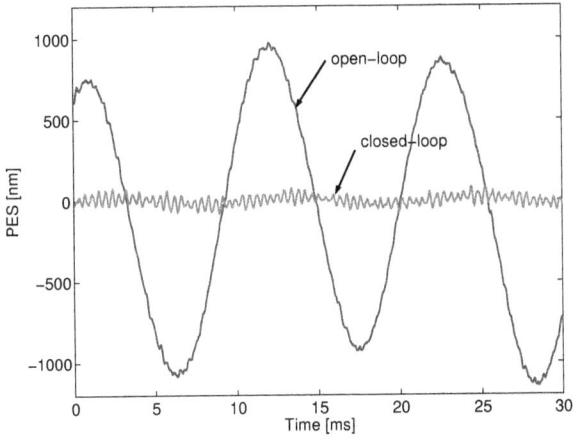

Figure 6.17: Time trace of the measured PES

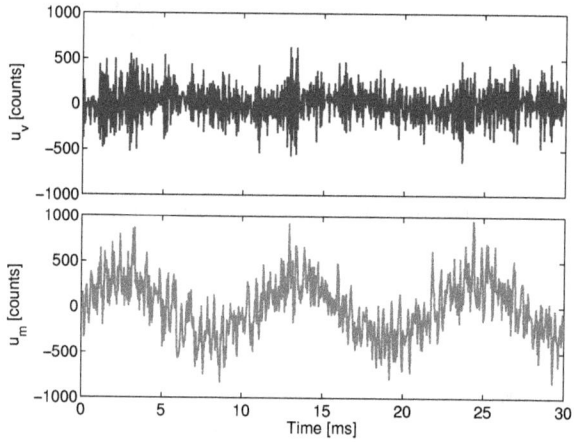

Figure 6.18: Time traces of the control inputs u_v and u_m

Chapter 7

Conclusions

In this book, robust controller design methodologies were developed, and simulation and experimental studies were carried out for dual-stage servo systems in hard disk drives.

A detailed dual-stage plant model was constructed. This model has a MEMS MA which can be either rotational or translational. The suspension was instrumented to have a strain sensor for detection of vibrations excited by airflow turbulence. The coupling effect of the translational MA was explicitly modeled. An uncertainty model, which includes both real parametric and complex multiplicative uncertainty, was established. Multirate sampler and hold were used in order to improve system performance.

Two SISO design methodologies were explored: the SD method and the PQ method. High rate inner loop damping compensators were first closed around the plant, then low rate tracking controllers were designed. Three MIMO design methodologies were explored: mixed H_2/H_∞, mixed H_2/μ, and robust H_2. All of the three methods consider robust stability explicitly, and the last one optimizes the worst-case performance directly. Detailed comparison showed that the translational MA has the advantage of suspension vibration attenuation over the rotational one. SISO designs are straightforward to design and easy to implement and tune, while MIMO designs behave better in both nominal performance and performance robustness.

Experiments were conducted on two MA samples, and on a prototype dual-stage system with one of the two MAs. The coupling effect of the MAs and airflow excited MA vibration were estimated, validating the dual-stage actuator model used in the simulation. System identification was performed on that dual-stage system. With only the PES measurable, a preliminary design was conducted using the PQ method. Experimental results of the closed-loop system showed that the dual-stage system is functioning. Better performance is expected if the information about suspension vibration, y_p, and the MA relative motion, y_m, are also available.

Appendix A

Derivation of LMIs for Mixed H_2/H_∞ Synthesis

Here, we present the derivation of LMIs for the mixed H_2/H_∞ design method presented in Chapter 4. These LMIs can be derived using the ideas of congruent transformation and nonlinear change of variables [47][50].

A.1 For Linear Time-Invariant (LTI) Systems

Consider the general form of an LTI discrete system as defined in (2.22).

$$
\begin{bmatrix} z_\Delta \\ z_2 \\ y \end{bmatrix} = \left[\begin{array}{c|ccc} A & B_\Delta & B_2 & B_u \\ \hline C_\Delta & D_{\Delta\Delta} & D_{\Delta 2} & D_{\Delta u} \\ C_2 & D_{2\Delta} & D_{22} & D_{2u} \\ C_y & D_{y\Delta} & D_{y2} & 0 \end{array} \right] \begin{bmatrix} w_\Delta \\ w_2 \\ u \end{bmatrix},
$$

The dimensions for A, z_Δ, z_2, w_2, y and u are n_p, n_Δ, n_{z_2}, n_{w_2}, n_y and n_u, respectively. Suppose we have also designed a dynamic output feedback controller for the above system

$$
u = \left[\begin{array}{c|c} K_A & K_B \\ \hline K_C & K_D \end{array} \right] y, \tag{A.1}
$$

where the dimension of K_A is n_k. The closed-loop system with the output $[z_\Delta^T \, z_2^T]^T$ from the input $[w_\Delta^T \, w_2^T]^T$ can be written as

$$
\begin{aligned}
G_{cl} &= \left[\begin{array}{c|c} A_{cl} & B_{cl} \\ \hline C_{cl} & D_{cl} \end{array} \right] \\
&= \left[\begin{array}{cc|cc} A + B_u K_D C_y & B_u K_C & B_\Delta + B_u K_D D_{y\Delta} & B_2 + B_u K_D D_{y2} \\ K_B C_y & K_A & K_B D_{y\Delta} & K_B D_{y2} \\ \hline C_\Delta + D_{\Delta u} K_D C_y & D_{\Delta u} K_C & D_{\Delta\Delta} + D_{\Delta u} K_D D_{y\Delta} & D_{\Delta u} K_D D_{y2} \\ C_2 + D_{2u} K_D C_y & D_{2u} K_C & D_{2u} K_D D_{y\Delta} & D_{22} + D_{2u} K_D D_{y2} \end{array} \right].
\end{aligned} \tag{A.2}
$$

Define G_{cl2} as the closed-loop transfer function from w_2 to z_2, and $G_{cl\Delta}$ the closed-loop transfer function from w_Δ to z_Δ. They can be readily constructed by extracting relevant entries from G_{cl}.

Lemma 1. (H_2 norm condition.)

For the closed-loop system (A.2), the inequality $\|G_{z_2 w_2}\|_2^2 < \gamma_2$ holds, if and only if there exist positive definite matrices P_2 and W such that the following LMIs are feasible

$$\text{trace}(W) < \gamma_2 , \tag{A.3}$$

$$\begin{bmatrix} W & C_{cl2} P_2 & D_{cl2} \\ * & P_2 & 0 \\ * & * & I \end{bmatrix} > 0, \tag{A.4}$$

$$\begin{bmatrix} P_2 & A_{cl2} P_2 & B_{cl2} \\ * & P_2 & 0 \\ * & * & I \end{bmatrix} > 0, \tag{A.5}$$

where the symbol "*" denotes the transpose of the corresponding element at its transposed position.

Lemma 2. (H_∞ norm condition.)

For the closed-loop system (A.2), the inequality $\|G_{z_\Delta w_\Delta}\|_\infty^2 < 1$ holds if and only if there exists a positive definite matrix P_∞ such that

$$\begin{bmatrix} P_\infty & A_{cl\Delta} & B_{cl\Delta} & 0 \\ * & P_\infty & 0 & P_\infty C_{cl\Delta}^T \\ * & * & I & D_{cl\Delta}^T \\ * & * & * & I \end{bmatrix} > 0. \tag{A.6}$$

A mixed H_2/H_∞ optimization problem can be formed by combining conditions (A.3)-(A.6). It is seen that for each individual condition, either H_2 or H_∞, P_2 and P_∞ can be different. However, for the mixed optimization problem, we must impose the constraint

$$P_2 = P_\infty = P . \tag{A.7}$$

This restriction recovers convexity of the mixed optimization problem, and the resulting problem can therefore be handled by LMI optimization [50]. The price of this constraint is that certain conservatism is thus brought into the design.

Assuming the uniform variable P, we now partition P and P^{-1} into blocks as

$$P = \begin{bmatrix} Y & N \\ N^T & * \end{bmatrix}, \quad P^{-1} = \begin{bmatrix} X & M \\ M^T & * \end{bmatrix}.$$

Then we have

$$MN^T = I - XY . \tag{A.8}$$

We also define two transformation matrices

$$\Pi_1 := \begin{bmatrix} X & I \\ M^T & 0 \end{bmatrix}, \quad \Pi_2 := \begin{bmatrix} I & Y \\ 0 & N^T \end{bmatrix}. \tag{A.9}$$

It is readily verified that

$$P\Pi_1 = \Pi_2\,,$$
$$\Pi_1^T P\Pi_1 = \Pi_1^T \Pi_2 = \begin{bmatrix} X & I \\ I & Y \end{bmatrix}. \tag{A.10}$$

We need to define some nonlinear changes of controller variables as follows:

$$\hat{K}_A := X(A + B_u K_D C_y)Y + XB_u K_C N^T + MK_B C_y Y + MK_A N^T\,,$$
$$\hat{K}_B := XB_u K_D + MK_B\,,$$
$$\hat{K}_C := K_D C_y Y + K_C N^T\,, \tag{A.11}$$
$$\hat{K}_D := K_D\,.$$

When applied to those initial LMIs, the above similarity transformations convert the LMIs from analysis to synthesis, and a controller can therefore be solved for.

Applying similarity transformation and variable change to (A.4) leads to

$$\begin{bmatrix} I & & \\ & \Pi_1^T & \\ & & I \end{bmatrix} \begin{bmatrix} W & C_{\text{cl2}}P & D_{\text{cl2}} \\ * & P & 0 \\ * & * & I \end{bmatrix} \begin{bmatrix} I & & \\ & \Pi_1 & \\ & & I \end{bmatrix} > 0\,,$$

$$\Rightarrow \begin{bmatrix} W & C_2 + D_{yu}\hat{K}_D C_y & C_2 Y + D_{2u}\hat{K}_C & D_{22} + D_{2u}\hat{K}_D D_{y2} \\ * & X & I & 0 \\ * & * & Y & 0 \\ * & * & * & I \end{bmatrix} > 0\,. \tag{A.12}$$

Similarly from (A.5) we have

$$\begin{bmatrix} \Pi_1^T & & \\ & \Pi_1^T & \\ & & I \end{bmatrix} \begin{bmatrix} P & A_{\text{cl2}}P & B_{\text{cl2}} \\ * & P & 0 \\ * & * & I \end{bmatrix} \begin{bmatrix} \Pi_1 & & \\ & \Pi_1 & \\ & & I \end{bmatrix} > 0\,,$$

$$\Rightarrow \begin{bmatrix} X & I & XA + \hat{K}_B C_y & \hat{K}_A & XB_2 + \hat{K}_B D_{y2} \\ * & Y & A + B_u\hat{K}_D C_y & AY + B_u\hat{K}_C & B_2 + B_u\hat{K}_D D_{y2} \\ * & * & X & I & 0 \\ * & * & * & Y & 0 \\ * & * & * & * & I \end{bmatrix} > 0\,. \tag{A.13}$$

And (A.6) can be converted into

$$\begin{bmatrix} \Pi_1^T & & & \\ & \Pi_1^T & & \\ & & I & \\ & & & I \end{bmatrix} \begin{bmatrix} P & A_{\text{cl}\Delta} & B_{\text{cl}\Delta} & 0 \\ * & P & 0 & PC_{\text{cl}\Delta}^T \\ * & * & I & D_{\text{cl}\Delta}^T \\ * & * & * & I \end{bmatrix} \begin{bmatrix} \Pi_1 & & & \\ & \Pi_1 & & \\ & & I & \\ & & & I \end{bmatrix} > 0$$

$$\Rightarrow \begin{bmatrix} X & I & XA + \hat{K}_B C_y & \hat{K}_A & XB_\Delta + \hat{K}_B D_{y\Delta} & 0 \\ * & Y & A + B_u\hat{K}_D C_y & AY + B_u\hat{K}_C & B_\Delta + B_u\hat{K}_D D_{y\Delta} & 0 \\ * & * & X & I & 0 & C_\Delta^T + C_y^T\hat{K}_D^T D_{\Delta u}^T \\ * & * & * & Y & 0 & YC_\Delta^T + \hat{K}_C^T D_{\Delta u}^T \\ * & * & * & * & I & D_{\Delta\Delta}^T + D_{y\Delta}^T\hat{K}_D^T D_{\Delta u}^T \\ * & * & * & * & * & I \end{bmatrix} > 0\,. \tag{A.14}$$

By solving the optimization problem

$$\text{min trace}\{W\},$$
$$\text{subject to} \quad (A.12), (A.13), \text{and} (A.14), \tag{A.15}$$

we obtain the following decision variables: positive definite matrices W, X, Y, and generic matrices $\hat{K}_A$, $\hat{K}_B$, $\hat{K}_C$, and $\hat{K}_D$.

For the purpose of controller construction, we solve (A.8) for M and N. Then the actual controller can be derived from (A.11) as

$$K_D = \hat{K}_D,$$
$$K_C = \left(\hat{K}_C - \hat{K}_D C_y Y \right) N^{-T},$$
$$K_B = M^{-1}(\hat{K}_B - X B_2 \hat{K}_D), \tag{A.16}$$
$$K_A = M^{-1} \left(\hat{K}_A - X \left(A + B_u \hat{K}_D C_y \right) Y - X B_u K_C N^T - M K_B C_y Y \right) N^{-T}.$$

By introducing a few more decision variables [47][7], extensions can be made to the LMIs for H_2 and H_∞ norm conditions, . These additional variables provide more flexibility to exploit all degrees of freedom allowed by the norm conditions. Therefore, the resulting controller will be expected to be less conservative compared to the one presented here. The price of these extensions is that more decision variables and hence more computation time are needed to solve these LMIs.

A.2   For Periodically Time-Varying Systems

Based on the single-rate MIMO design methodology for LTI systems, there is a systematic way of incorporating multirateness into the design process. It is already shown that we can design a dynamic LTI controller (4.31) for the system (4.30) for both H_2 and H_∞ norm optimization. For simplicity, first define

$$M_Z := Z^T M Z, \tag{A.17}$$

for a stacked block-diagonal matrix $\boldsymbol{M}$ and a cyclic matrix Z with appropriate sizes. Note that $\boldsymbol{M}_Z$ is also block-diagonal.

Based on the results presented in Section A.1, we can readily derive all LMIs that correspond to (A.12), (A.13) and (A.14), by performing the following three steps.

1. Replace all system matrices and decision variables by their stacked form as defined in (4.28) and (4.33). Note that this replacement renders all entries in the resulting LMIs block-diagonal.

2. In (A.11), (A.13) and (A.14), replace $\boldsymbol{A}$, $\boldsymbol{B}$, $\boldsymbol{K}_A$ and $\boldsymbol{K}_B$, by $Z\boldsymbol{A}$, $Z\boldsymbol{B}$, $Z\boldsymbol{K}_A$ and $Z\boldsymbol{K}_B$, respectively. Note that this replacement renders $\hat{K}_A$ and $\hat{K}_B$ non-block-diagonal. However, it is easily verified that $\hat{\hat{K}}_A := Z\hat{K}_A$ and $\hat{\hat{K}}_B := Z\hat{K}_B$ are still block-diagonal.

3. Do the following two similarity transformations. Multiply (A.13) by diag$[Z^T, Z^T, I,$ $I, I]$ from the left and by diag$[Z, Z, I, I, I]$ from the right. Multiply (A.14) by diag$[Z^T, Z^T, I, I, I, I]$ from the left and by diag$[Z, Z, I, I, I, I]$ from the right.

After these transformations, we obtain the following LMIs for periodically a time-varying system:

$$\begin{bmatrix} W & C_2 + D_{yu}\hat{K}_D C_y & C_2 Y + D_{2u}\hat{K}_C & D_{22} + D_{2u}\hat{K}_D D_{y2} \\ * & X & I & 0 \\ * & * & Y & 0 \\ * & * & * & I \end{bmatrix} > 0. \qquad (A.18)$$

$$\begin{bmatrix} X_Z & I & X_Z A + \hat{K}_B C_y & \hat{K}_A & X_Z B_2 + \hat{K}_B D_{y2} \\ * & Y_Z & A + B_u \hat{K}_D C_y & AY + B_u \hat{K}_C & B_2 + B_u \hat{K}_D D_{y2} \\ * & * & X & I & 0 \\ * & * & * & Y & 0 \\ * & * & * & * & I \end{bmatrix} > 0. \qquad (A.19)$$

$$\begin{bmatrix} X_Z & I & X_Z A + \hat{K}_B C_y & \hat{K}_A & X_Z B_\Delta + \hat{K}_B D_{y\Delta} & 0 \\ * & Y_Z & A + B_u \hat{K}_D C_y & AY + B_u \hat{K}_C & B_\Delta + B_u \hat{K}_D D_{y\Delta} & 0 \\ * & * & X & I & 0 & C_\Delta^T + C_y^T \hat{K}_D^T D_{\Delta u}^T \\ * & * & * & Y & 0 & Y C_\Delta^T + \hat{K}_C^T D_{\Delta u}^T \\ * & * & * & * & I & D_{\Delta\Delta}^T + D_{y\Delta}^T \hat{K}_D^T D_{\Delta u}^T \\ * & * & * & * & * & I \end{bmatrix} > 0, \qquad (A.20)$$

where $\hat{K}_C := \hat{K}_C$, and $\hat{K}_D := \hat{K}_D$.

We then solve the optimization problem

$$\min \ \text{trace}\{W\}, \\ \text{subject to} \quad (A.18), (A.19), \text{ and } (A.20). \qquad (A.21)$$

After obtaining the decision variables, W, X, Y, $\hat{K}_A$, $\hat{K}_B$, $\hat{K}_C$, and $\hat{K}_D$, the final controller is obtained as follows:

$$\begin{aligned} K_D &= \hat{K}_D, \\ K_C &= \left(\hat{K}_C - K_D C_y Y\right) N^{-T}, \\ K_B &= M_Z^{-1}(\hat{K}_B - X_Z B_2 K_D), \\ K_A &= M_Z^{-1}\left(\hat{K}_A - X_Z\left(A + B_u K_D C_y\right) Y - X_Z B_u K_C N^T - M_Z K_B C_y Y\right) N^{-T}. \end{aligned} \qquad (A.22)$$

It is seen that the resulting controller matrices are still block-diagonal, since all matrices in the above equations are block-diagonal.

Appendix B

Balanced Truncation Model Reduction for Periodic Systems

The following results are from [58]. The reader is referred to that paper for more details. Consider a linear discrete-time T-periodic system

$$\begin{aligned} x_{k+1} &= A_k x_k + B_k u_k \\ y_k &= C_k x_k \,, \end{aligned} \tag{B.1}$$

where all A_k's have the same dimension n and all other matrices and vectors have compatible dimensions. It is noted that, the system (B.1) is just another representation of the periodically time-varying controller (4.34) with the D_k matrix omitted, since it will be kept intact after model reduction. The transition matrix of the system (B.1) is defined by

$$\Phi_A(j,i) := A_{j-1} A_{j-2} \cdots A_i \,, \tag{B.2}$$

then we define G_k and F_k as

$$G_k := \begin{bmatrix} B_{k-1} & A_{k-1} B_{k-2} & \cdots & \Phi_A(k, i+1) B_i & \cdots \end{bmatrix}, \tag{B.3}$$

$$F_k := \begin{bmatrix} C_k \\ C_{k+1} A_k \\ \vdots \\ C_i \Phi_A(i, k) \\ \vdots \end{bmatrix}. \tag{B.4}$$

The reachability and observability Gramians are respectively defined as

$$P_k = G_k G_k^T \geq 0 \,, \tag{B.5}$$

$$Q_k = F_k^T F_k \geq 0 \,. \tag{B.6}$$

For an asymptotically stable periodic system, the two Gramians are nonnegative definite and satisfy nonnegative discrete periodic Lyapunov equations

$$P_Z = A P A^T + B B^T \,, \tag{B.7}$$

$$Q = A^T Q_Z^T A + C^T C \,, \tag{B.8}$$

where the cyclic matrix Z was defined in (4.29), $\boldsymbol{A} := \text{diag}[A_0, A_1, \ldots, A_{T-1}]$, and $\boldsymbol{P}_Z := Z^T \boldsymbol{P} Z$.

Perform Cholesky factorizations of Gramians

$$\boldsymbol{P} = \boldsymbol{S}^T \boldsymbol{S}, \quad \boldsymbol{Q} = \boldsymbol{R}^T \boldsymbol{R}, \tag{B.9}$$

then do the singular value decomposition

$$\boldsymbol{R}\boldsymbol{S}^T = \boldsymbol{U}\boldsymbol{\Sigma}\boldsymbol{V}^T. \tag{B.10}$$

Assume that the remaining model order at time k is r_k, then do the following partitions

$$U_k = \begin{bmatrix} U_{k,1} & U_{k,2} \end{bmatrix}, \quad V_k = \begin{bmatrix} V_{k,1} & V_{k,2} \end{bmatrix}, \quad k = 0, \ldots, T-1, \tag{B.11}$$

where $U_{k,1} \in \mathbb{R}^{n \times r_k}$, and $V_{k,1} \in \mathbb{R}^{n \times r_k}$.

Consider the QR decompositions

$$\boldsymbol{S}^T \boldsymbol{V}_1 = \boldsymbol{T}\boldsymbol{X}, \quad \boldsymbol{R}^T \boldsymbol{U}_1 = \boldsymbol{Z}\boldsymbol{Y}, \tag{B.12}$$

where $\boldsymbol{X}$ and $\boldsymbol{Y}$ are nonsingular matrices, and $\boldsymbol{T}$ and $\boldsymbol{Z}$ are matrices with orthogonal columns. With the already defined $\boldsymbol{T}$, we define the corresponding $\boldsymbol{L}$ as

$$\boldsymbol{L} = (\boldsymbol{Z}^T \boldsymbol{T})^{-1} \boldsymbol{Z}^T. \tag{B.13}$$

The matrices $\boldsymbol{L}$ and $\boldsymbol{T}$ are called the *truncation* matrices. Then the reduced system can be computed

$$\boldsymbol{A}_r = \boldsymbol{L}_Z \boldsymbol{A}\boldsymbol{T}, \quad \boldsymbol{B}_r = \boldsymbol{L}_Z \boldsymbol{B}, \quad \boldsymbol{C}_r = \boldsymbol{C}\boldsymbol{T}. \tag{B.14}$$

Bibliography

[1] D. Abramovitch and G. Franklin. A brief history of disk drive control. *IEEE Control System Magazine*, 22:28–42, Jul 2002.

[2] S. Arya, Y.-S. Lee, W.-M. Lu, M. Staudenmann, and M. Hatchett. Piezo-based milliactuator on a partially etched suspension. *IEEE Trans. Magnetics*, 37(2):934–939, 2001.

[3] S.-E. Baek and S.-H. Lee. Vibration rejection control for disk drives by acceleration feedforward control. In *Proc. 38th IEEE Conf. on Decision and Control*, Dec. 1999.

[4] G. J. Balas, J. C. Doyle, K. Glover, A. Packard, and R. Smith. *μ-Analysis and Synthesis Toolbox for use with MATLAB*. MUSYN Inc. and The MathWorks, Inc., USA, 1995.

[5] H. W. Bode. *Network Analysis and Feedback Amplifier Design*. Van Nostrand, New York, 1945.

[6] T.-L. Chen. *Design and fabrication of PZT-actuated silicon suspensions for hard disk drives*. PhD thesis, Dept. of Mechanical Engineering, Univ. of California at Berkeley, 2001.

[7] C. Du, L. Xie, J.-N. Teoh, and G. Guo. An improved mixed H_2/H_∞ control design for hard disk drives. *IEEE Trans. Control Systems Technology*, 13(5):832–839, 2005.

[8] G. E. Dullerud and S. Lall. A new approach for analysis and synthesis of time-varying systems. *IEEE Trans. Automat. Control*, 44(8):1486–1497, 1999.

[9] R. Ehrlich and D. Curran. Major HDD TMR sources and projected scaling with TPI. *IEEE Trans. Magnetics*, 35(2):885–891, 1999.

[10] P. Gahinet, A. Nemirovske, A. J. Laub, and M. Chilali. *LMI Control Toolbox*. The MathWorks, Inc., USA, 1995.

[11] J.S. Griesbach, R.B. Evans, and W.C. Messner. Piezoelectric microactuator for dual-stage control. *IEEE Trans. Magnetics*, 35:977–981, 1999.

[12] H. M. Gross. *Off-track vibrations of the read-write heads in HDDs*. PhD thesis, Dept. of Mechanical Engineering, Univ. of California at Berkeley, 2003.

[13] Y. Gu and M. Tomizuka. Digital redesign and multirate control for motion control. In *Proc. Int. Workshop on Advanced Motion Control*, pages 246–251, 2000.

[14] L. Guo and Y.-J. D. Chen. Disk flutter and its impact on HDD servo performance. *IEEE Trans. Magnetics*, 37(2):866–870, 2001.

[15] L. Guo, H. S. Lee, A. Hudson, and S.-H. Chen. A comprehensive time-domain simulation for HDD TPI prediction and mechanical/servo enhancement. *IEEE Trans. Magnetics*, 35(2):879–884, 1999.

[16] T. Hara and M. Tomizuka. Multirate controller for HDDs with redesign of state estimator. In *Proc. American Control Conf.*, pages 3033–3037, 1998.

[17] D. Hernandez, S.-S. Park, R. Horowitz, and A. K. Packard. Dual-stage track-following servo design for hard disk derives. In *Proc. American Control Conf.*, pages 4188–4121, 1999.

[18] HGST.   Perpendicular   recording.   http://www.hitachigst.com/hdd/ research/recording_head/pr/index.html, 2005.

[19] T. Hirano, L.-S. Fan, W.Y. Lee, J. Hong, W. Imaino, S. Pattanaik, S. Chan, R. Horowitz, S. Aggarwal, and D.A. Horsley. High-bandwidth high-accuracy rotary microactuators for magnetic disk drive tracking servos. *IEEE/ASME Trans. Mechatronics*, 3:156–165, 1998.

[20] T. Hirano, M. White, H. Yang, K. Scott, S. Pattanaik, S. Arya, and F.-Y. Huang. A moving-slider MEMS actuator for high-bandwidth HDD tracking. In *Proc. of Intermag*, volume 3, pages 2535–2540, Anaheim, CA, 2003.

[21] D. Horsley, N. Wongkomet, R. Horowitz, and A. Pisano. Precision positioning using a microfabricated electrostatic actuator. *IEEE Trans. Magnetics*, 35(2):993–999, 1999.

[22] X. Hu, W. Guo, T. Huang, and B. M. Chen. Discrete-time LQG/LTR dual-stage controller design and implementation for high track density HDDs. In *Proc. American Control Conf.*, pages 4111–4115, 1999.

[23] F. Y. Huang, T. Semba, W. Imaino, and F. Lee. Active damping in HDD actuator. *IEEE Trans. Magnetics*, 37(2):847–849, 2001.

[24] X. Huang and R. Horowitz. Robust controller design of a dual-stage disk drive servo system with an instrumented suspension. *IEEE Trans. Magnetics*, 8(5):194–200, 2005.

[25] X. Huang, R. Horowitz, and Y. Li. Track-following control with active vibration damping and compensation of a dual-stage servo system. *Microsystem Technologies*, 10:1194–1205, 2005.

[26] X. Huang, R. Horowitz, and Yunfeng Li. Design and analysis of robust track-following controllers for dual-stage servo systems with an instrumented suspension. In *Proc. American Control Conf.*, pages 1126–1131, 2005.

[27] X. Huang, R. Nagamune, and R. Horowitz. A comparison of multirate robust track-following control synthesis techniques for dual-stage and multi-sensing servo systems in HDDs. In *Proc. American Control Conf.*, 2006.

[28] Y. Huang, M. Banther, P. D. Mathur, and W. Messner. Design and analysis of a high bandwidth disk drive servo system using an instrumeted suspension. *IEEE/ASME Trans. Mechatronics*, 4(2):196–206, 1999.

[29] S. Kanev, C. Scherer, M. Verhaegen, and B. De Schutter. Robust output-feedback controller design via local BMI optimization. *Automatica*, 40(7):1115–1127, 2004.

[30] H. Kuwajima and K. Matsuoka. Thin film piezoelectric dual-stage actuator for HDDs. In *InterMag Europe, Session BS04*, 2002.

[31] S. Lall and G. Dullerud. An LMI solution to the robust synthesis problem for multirate sampled-data systems. *Automatica*, 37(12):1909–1922, 2001.

[32] Y. Li. *Dual-stage servo control and active vibration compensation in magnetic HDDs.* PhD thesis, Dept. of Mechanical Engineering, Univ. of California at Berkeley, 2003.

[33] Y. Li and R. Horowitz. Active suspension vibration control with dual-stage actuators in hard disk drives. In *Proc. American Control Conf.*, pages 2786–2791, 2001.

[34] Y. Li and R. Horowitz. Mechatronics of electrostatic microactuators for computer disk drive dual-stage servo systems. *IEEE/ASME Trans. Mechatronics*, 6(2):111–121, 2001.

[35] Y. Li and R. Horowitz. Active vibration control of a PZT actuated suspension in hard disk drives. In *Proc. American Control Conf.*, pages 1366–1371, 2002.

[36] Y. Li and R. Horowitz. Design and testing of track-following controllers for dual-stage servo systems with pzt actuated suspensions. *Microsystem Technologies*, 8:194–205, 2002.

[37] Y. Li, F. Marcassa, R. Horowitz, R. Oboe, and R. Evans. Track-following control with active vibration damping of a PZT-actuated suspension dual-stage servo system. In *Proc. American Control Conf.*, pages 2553–2559, 2003.

[38] M. Mita, H. Toshiyoshi, and H. Fujita. Electrostatic piggyback microactuators for head element positioning. In *Proc. ASME/IEEE Asia Pacific Magnetic Recording Conf.*, Singapore, Aug. 28-29 2002.

[39] C. Mohtadi and M. A. Dphil. Bode's integral theorem for discrete-time systems. *IEE Proc. D*, 137, 1990.

[40] K. Mori, T. Munemoto, H. Otsuki, Y. Yamaguchi, and K. Akagi. A dual-stage magnetic disk drive actuator using a piezoelectric device for a high track density. *IEEE Trans. Magnetics*, 27(6):5298–5300, 1991.

[41] R. Nagamune, X. Huang, and R. Horowitz. Multirate track-following control with robust stability for dual-stage multi-sensing servo systems in HDDs. In *Proc. IEEE Conf. on Decision and Control*, Dec 2005.

[42] R. Nagamune, X. Huang, and R. Horowitz. Robust H_2 synthesis for dual-stage multi-sensing track-following servo systems in HDDs. In *Proc. American Control Conf.*, 2006.

[43] R. Oboe. Use of low-cost MEMS accelerometers for vibration compensation in hard disk drives. In *Proc. of the 6th Intl. Workshop on Advanced Motion Control*, pages 485–489, 2000.

[44] K. Oldham, X. Huang, and R. Horowitz. Design, fabrication, and control of a high-aspect ratio microactuator for vibration suppression in a hard disk drive. In *Proc. of 16th IFAC World Congress*, Prague, Czech, July 2005.

[45] K. Oldham, S. Kon, and R. Horowitz. Fabricatin and optimal strain sensor placement in an instrumented disk drive suspension for vibration suppression. Technical Report 10, CML Blue Report, Dept. of Mechanical Engineering, U. C. Berkeley, Oct. 2003.

[46] K. Oldham, S. Kon, and R. Horowitz. Fabrication and optimal strain sensor placement in an instrumented disk drive suspension for vibration suppression. In *Proc. American Control Conf.*, pages 1855–1860, 2004.

[47] M. C. De Oliveira, J. C. Geromel, and J. Bernussou. Extended H_2 and H_∞ norm characterizations and controller parametrizations for discrete-time systems. *Int. J. Control*, 75(9):666–679, 2002.

[48] F. Paganini. Frequency domain conditions for robust H_2 performance. *IEEE Trans. Automat. Control*, 44(1):95–103, 1999.

[49] S. Pannu and R. Horowitz. Increased disturbance rejection for hard disk drives using accelerometers. *The J. of Info. Storage and Processing Systems*, 1:95–103, 1999.

[50] C. Scherer, P. Gahinet, and M. Chilali. Multiobjective output feedback control via LMI optimization. *IEEE Trans. Automatic Control*, 42(7):896–911, 1997.

[51] S. J. Schroeck and W. C. Messner. On controller design for linear time-invariant dual-input single-output systems. In *Proc. American Control Conf.*, pages 4122–4126, 1999.

[52] T. Semba. An h_∞ design method for a multirate servo controller and applications to a high density hard disk drive. In *Proc. 40th IEEE Conf. on Decision and Control*, pages 4693–4698, 2001.

[53] T. Semba, T. Hirano, and L.-S. Fan. Dual-stage servo controller for HDD using MEMS actuator. *IEEE Trans. Magnetics*, 35(2):2271–2273, 1999.

[54] D. H. Shim, H. S. Lee, and L. Guo. Mixed-objective optimization of track-following controllers using linear matrix inequalities. In *Proc. of American Control Conf.*, pages 4323–4328, 2003.

[55] P. Srikrishna and K. Kasetty. Predicting TMR from disk vibration of alternate substrate materials. *IEEE Trans. Magnetics*, 36(1):847–849, 2000.

[56] J. F. Sturm. *Using Sedumi 1.05, A MATLAB Toolbox for Optimization over Symmetric Cones*. 2001.

[57] H. Toshiyoshi. Electrostatic piggyback microactuators for head element positioning. http://toshi.fujita3.iis.u-tokyo.ac.jp, 2002.

[58] A. Varga. Balanced truncation model reduction of periodic systems. In *Proc. 39th IEEE Conf. on Decision and Control*, pages 2379–2384, 2000.

[59] M. White and M. Tomizuka. Increased disturbance rejection in magnetic disk drives by acceleration feedforward control. In *Proc. 13th World Congress of IFAC*, San Francisco, CA, USA, July 1996.

[60] M. T. White and T. Hirano. Use of relative position signal for microactuators in hard disk drives. In *Proc. of American Control Conf.*, pages 2535–2540, 2003.

[61] S.-C. Wu and M. Tomizuka. Multirate digital control with interlacing and its application to hard disk drive servo. In *Proc. of American Control Conf.*, pages 4347–4352, 2003.

[62] S.-C. Wu and M. Tomizuka. Performance and aliasing analysis of multirate digital controllers with interlacing. In *Proc. of American Control Conf.*, pages 3514–3519, 2004.

[63] T. Yamaguchi. Modelling and control of a disk file head positioning system. *Proc. Institution of Mechanical Engineers*, 215:549–567, 2001.

[64] Y. Yamaguchi. Flow-induced vibration of magnetic head suspension in HDDs. *IEEE Trans. Magnetics*, 22:1022–1024, 1986.

www.ingramcontent.com/pod-product-compliance
Lightning Source LLC
Chambersburg PA
CBHW052016230326
41598CB00078B/3518